Encyclopaedia of Commerce and Management 12

MATERIALS MANAGEMENT

Editors

ASIT K. GHOSH
PREM KUMAR

ANMOL PUBLICATIONS PVT. LTD.
NEW DELHI-110 002 (INDIA)

ANMOL PUBLICATIONS PVT LTD
4374/4B, Ansari Road, Daryaganj
New Delhi-110 002

Reprint 1997
Reprint, 2000
ISBN 81-7041-366-4

PRINTED IN INDIA

Published by J. L. Kumar for Anmol Publications Pvt Ltd, New Delhi-110 002 and Printed at Tarun Offset, Press, Delhi.

Preface

The efficient and optimum control of production functions includes the mechanism of materials management to ensure quick, timely and correct in flow of resources into the production chain and a thorough manitoring of all finished goods as well as waste and by-products. The many aspects of production control including supply, purchase, quality control and loading of materials are discussed in the papers, articles, discussion notes, etc., included in this compilation. The authors are exports in their respective areas and other papers—presented at seminars or prepared by organisational teams—are equally valuable in throwing light on the ways and means of efficient and optimum materials management. The Supply function in the production function is not generally given the attention it deserves and it is hoped that the papers included in this volume will be useful for all students and scholars as well as teachers in university, college and organisational department of management, business economics and purchase as well as supply and disposal whigs of companies and industrial/manufacturing units.

Contents

1

Introduction

The principles of production planning, including materials management and control are general; they apply to all branches, products, types of production and sizes of companies. Materials Management in the modern corporate enterprise will thus be determined by product decisions, production planning and related aspects.

The methods of application will vary however, depending mainly on the following factors:

1. Whether products are special purpose of standard products.
2. Whether products are made to customer order or to stock.
3. Whether the type of production is single project, intermittent or continuous.

These factors are more or less inter-related as shown below. In particular it may be stated that the type of products and the type of orders determine the type of production.

Type of Product	*Type of Production*	*Type of Order*
Special purpose→	Single project	↖ ↙ Customer orders
	Intermittent	
standard ↗ ↘	continuous	↖ ↙ stock delivery ord.

The different characteristics of the three types of production will be discussed in some details.

1. SINGLE PROJECT TYPE OF PRODUCTION

By single project type of production is meant the making of special products in small quantities, and that no one order is expected to be repeated.

Examples : shipbuilding, turbines, special transformers, special transportation and handling equipment, etc.

In spite of the typical non-uniformity of products being made in this type of production there are certain common characteristics that have some bearing on the planning and control methods to be employed.

In general, the prodncts are costly and complicated. In process time is considerable.

Companies where this type of production is prevailing are usually working on a price-bid basis.

It is rather normal for these companies to be out of balance as far as workload is concerned.

A mixture of overtime work in one department and overcapacity in another may result. In generaal machine utilisation is low.

Most machines in these companies are general purpose machines. This means that operations are rather inaffective and that set-up time per unit is considerable.

Process layout is used invariably in these companies.

Highly skilled labourers are often required in this type of operations.

A great variety of jobs and frequent change-over in any machine necessitate these conditions.

The number of instructions necessary is high in this type of production.

This is true for production as well as service functions.

A sufficient number of wide aisles is required.

Still it is rather common to find disorder and crowded work areas in this type of production.

Advantages of Single Project Type of Production

Flexibility in choice of products because of layout, types of machines installed, transportation system, the skills of the works.

Low initial investments in machinery.

Disadvantages of Single Projcct Type of Production

High labour and machine cost per unit.

High inventories.

Considerable floor space required.

Much clerical work required.

2. INTERMITTENT PRODUCTION

By intermittent production we mean the making of a limited number of rather standardised products on a lot-basis, and where lots are repeated more or less regularly.

Examples: most customers goods made for a limited markct, such as household appliances, production equipment as hand tools, machine tools etc.

The only essential difference between single-project and intermittent production lies in the fact that the number of units produced in intermittent production is higher and that these products are being made repeatedly.

The characteristics of intermittent production are not essentially different from the single-project; it is rather a matter of the degree in which they are present.

This difference in degree however, may have a great effect on the production control procedures used compared to those to be used in the single-project type of production.

3. CONTINUOUS PRODUCTION (LINE PRODUCTION)

Continuous production exists where the material moves continuously and at a uniform rate through a sequence of balanced operations towards completion.

Examples: automobile assembly.

The essential characteristic of continuous production is the large volume and small variety of products made.

Balanced capacity of successive machines is essential to continuous production

Production layout is used in most instances.

The machines used in continuous production are special-purpose machines rather than general-purpose machines.

Continuous production does not call for highly skilled workers and foremen as does the intermittent and single-project type of manufacture.

Few job instructions are necessary in continuous production.

Low inventory of materials in process compared to output.

Materials are often moved on conveyor and little storage space is required.

Advantages of Continuous Production

Low unit costs of product due to low investment in inventory, special-purpose machines of high output, use of semi-skilled operators: good utilisation of floor space, low operating costs of transportation equipment.

Disadvantages of Continuous Production

Inflexibility: Considerable expenses involved in changing of product or product design due to layout and special-purpose machines.

Vulnerability to work stoppages.

Rigidity of the rate of output.

These different types of production call for different production control procedures, while there are considerable similarity of the procedure used within each type of production.

TYPES OF PRODUCTION CONTROL

Variations in manufacturing do not change the need for performing production control functions, but they do change the frequency with which certain functions must be performed. It is necessary to adapt production control procedures to suit the situation in each company.

We have already discussed the classification of industry into two main groups, intermittent and continuous. The intermittent group must perform production control functions in the face of continual change, regardless of the kind of product made. The type of control used is called "order" control. Continuous industries, on the other hand, carry out production control functions under conditions of extreme repetition and little variety. The control system is here much simpler. This type is called "flow" or "rate" control. A type of control combining the two main types is used by companies in which different lots of materials must be followed through a fixed set of operations. Some companies use the term "block" control, others "batch" control, while a third group uses "load" control.

Order Control

The following is a list of some of the characteristics of order control:

1. Many small lots of goods or "orders" are being produced simultaneously and need to be controlled individually.
2. There is little chance of long-time planning and to use old plans over again on products made to customers' orders.
3. A number is usually assigned to each order so the accounting department can keep track of the costs.
4. The order number is used for identifying the order throughout each department.
5. Order control permits the necessary instructions and directions to be made up and sent to the factory and applied to each lot.

Flow Control

Characteristics of flow control:

1. All materials and parts flow through production at a constant rate, and there is no charge in the kind of products being made from one day to the next.
2. No necessity of production control in the day-to-day work.
3. Less frequent reports to production control.
4. No need to instruct worker daily.
5. Production control must instruct the producing departments as to the planned rate of production and receive their reports (weekly) showing the actual rate accomplished.

Block, Batch or Load Control

Between intermittent and continuous industries lie similar process industries, whose processes are like continuous industries but whose control problems resemble those in intermittent production.

"Block" control is used in industries where the plant capacity is parcelled out or blocked out for use in producing certain large orders or groups of small orders. This system is used in factories making men's suits and in shoe factories.

"Batch" control is used in chemical process industries where each batch (or mix) is controlled separately.

"Load" control is necessary in continuous industries turning out large quantities of somewhat standard products. The book publishing industry is an example of this type. The variations in types of products (different books) make it necessary to cut the flow of products into separate segments which must be controlled.

Characteristic of load control :

1. Production operations are not carried on as smoothly as in continuous manufacturing.

2. There is seldom a perfect balance of capacity between consecutive operations.
3. Instructions concerning the kind and quantity of products to be made must be sent to every point where machines have to be adjusted.

Special Project Control

Heavy, large-size industrial equipment is often made up in sections in the factory and then moved to the point of use where the sections are assembled under the direction of the manufacturer's representatives. In this category belong ships, turboelectric generating equipment, bridges, etc. Such products are usually unique; only one, or a very few, of a kind are wanted. The product is of gigantic size, contains thousands of parts, takes months to produce, and involves large sums of money. Ordinary order control must be modified considerably to meet such production control needs. The terms "time schedule" or "co-ordinated effort" describe the control used. Segments of the work are planned in a general way, and finishing dates are set for the completion of major portions of the job. Close co-operation with the engineering department is mandatory since the engineering department often determines the final design of some parts after production is started.

Centralisation of Production Control Functions

Basic production control functions exist in all types and sizes of factories. There are, however, substantial differences in the degree to which the performance of these functions is concentrated in the hands of the central department.

Flow, block and load control are usually centralised to high degree. In order control where the form of control is more complex, there is some degree of decentralisation since it is very difficult to an effective job in a central office in carrying out all the detailed work.

Small companies (employing up to 100) ordinarily do not centralise production control. Most of the control work is done by the departments' foreman and the operators.

Some disadvantages of complete centralisation:

1. Slow to make emergency adjustments.
2. More clerical cost.
3. Frictions between department foremen and production control occur more frequently.
4. It is almost impossible for the production control department to know all details in every department.

Because of these disadvantages, in order control there should be some degree of decentralisation: that means, the foremen should do some control in his own department.

COST ESTIMATING IN PLANNING

Cost estimating in production planning is the task of determining the production costs, prior to actual production.

1. The Need for Cost Estimates

Accurate estimates are essential to the success of all companies. The estimates are serving the following purposes:

A. To submit price bids to customers before getting orders.
B. To obtain future costs of existing products where changes in sales volumes are expected or planned.
C. To determine expected selling price on new products or on products where changes in design are being made.

In general, cost estimates are even more important to companies producing to stock than to companies producing to customer's order, Product design and quality standards are set in accordance with an expected selling price, and if production costs prove to be higher than the estimate serious losses may result.

2. Basic Data Needed for Estimating

The following information is usually needed in order to make estimates:

A. Parts lists.

B. Operation lists.

C. Operation times.

D. Machines and equipment to be used.

3. Cost Items to be Estimated in Production Planning

In general, selling price is based on the cost of material, labour and various burden charges along with some measure of profit.

A. Cost of Material

Cost of material may be estimated with various degrees of accurancy, according to the requirement in each case.

Material costs are estimated by gross length, area or weight used per unit of product. The basic source of information will be the part lists. Costs may be determined from previous estimates, or the recorded amount of material used in the past for similar jobs run in the plant.

Costs of material may also be determined more accurately by analytical methods; *i.e.*, by actual measurement from drawings, models, etc.

Effect of waste and scrap is often very important in material cost estimates.

Examples: fitting of patterns, placing blanks in dies.

In exact material estimating can be a real source of loss. Material costs are becoming an ever-increasing percentage of the total cost because labour-saving machines tend to reduce labour costs.

Each industry will have its own way of estimating material cost, but a separate from for estimating these costs or a separate place on a prime cost form is often used.

A form will usually contain the following information:

Estimate number
Customer or department
Part name and number
Part drawing number
Final product name and number
Kind of material
Price of material
Actual quantity in part or unit plus price of same
Normal waste and scrap per unit plus price of same
Actual cost of material needed per part or unit
Material cost for number of part in order
(Signed by estimator).

B. Costs of Labour

Before any estimate can be made of the amount of labour required, the method of production must be known.

The basic source of information will be the operation list and the operation times. In addition, the following general information is needed:

1. Machine performance data.
2. Hourly rate of labour.

Sources for machine performance data should be a file containing all pertinent data regarding each machine or assembly stations, *i.e.* :

Essential dimensions

Speeds

Feeds

Production rates, etc.

Sources for labour rates are usually found in the personnel data cards filed in personnel or accounting department, giving rates of the different grades of labour being used.

C. Burden Charges

In addition to material and labour, cost estimates consider the factory overhead. This burden usually includes the following charges :

Depreciation

Interest

Maintenance

Heat

Light

Power etc.

In addition the factory burden includes its share of the administration buildings and personnel (administration charges may be distributed by accounting division in several ways, but each department will carry some portion of them).

4. Estimating Forms

The estimates should be recorded on forms showing all the main items included in the estimate.

Table 1.1 is an example of a form used for the labour and burden estimates.

Table 1.2 is a form to record summary of costs.

5. Notes

Cost is sometimes a poor basis for price, competitors may set the price level and problem will be how to design and make in order to sell at that price without loss.

The accuracy in estimating will depend on the sources of information available.

AUTHORITY TO MANUFACTURE

In general there is usually only a limited demand for any individual kind of finished products. Under ordinary conditions, sales are being made continually, products are constantly being demanded by the sales department and the factory is turning out products all the time. Because of the restricted market for any individual kind of products, however, the stream of products is not homogeneous.

The demand for some products declines while that for others increases, seasonal variations in demand may exist and may change, customers needs and wishes are subject to variation, etc.

This continuous shifting of demand requires that someone takes orders, observes inventories, evaluates trends and informs the factory what should be the contents of the stream of products to be turned out.

TABLE 1.1

Labour and Burden Estimates for Operations

On

Part Name.................Part No.................Drwg. No. ....Date........
For Customer or Dept......................Material...

Dept.	*Oper. No.*	*Operation Name*	*Machine Name and No.*	*Set-Up Analysis*				*Labour Analysis*				*Dept. Burden*		
				Set Up	*Rate*	*Cost*	*Dept. Sub Total*	*Out-put Per Hr.*	*Rate Per Hr.*	*Cost Per Unit*	*Dept. Sub Total*	*Sum of Lab-our and Set Up*	*Dept. Rate %*	*Burden Charge*
65	1	Set-up Lathe	Lathe No. 12	1/2	0.80	0.40								
65	2	Turn Outside Diameter	Lathe No. 12					300	0.60	0.20				
Quantity to be estimated...... Total														

Set-up=. . .
Labour=. . .
Burden=. . .
Total=per "unit"

Cost for. . . . . .pieces. . . . .
Estimated by. . . . .

TABLE 1.2

Total Estimated Cost of Materials, Labour and Burden

for

Product Name..............Part No.............Drwg. No...... ....Date...........

For Customer or Dept. ....Estimated Cost Per Unit of Product...........

Based on Order of...................Units.

Part No.	*Estimate No.*	*Part Name*	*Number of Part*	*Material Cost*	*Labour Cost*		*Prime Cost*	*Burden Charge*	*Total Cost*
					Set-Up	*Operation*			
Cost of all Parts Incl. Assembly									
Additional Tool Costs									
Total Costs									

Estimated by. . . . . .

1. Sources and Types of Authority

Two main types of authority exist:

Processing authority (how to make goods and perform operations).

Producing authority (when and how many of each kind to make).

Processing authority covers how to produce goods and applies to current and future orders unless specifically limited.

The original source of processing authority may be the engineering department, the industrial engineering department, work study department or production control department.

Processing authority is given in the form of bills of materials, routing sheets, drawings, specifications and instructions.

Processing authority is filed for future reference by production control department.

Old processing instructions are cancelled only when now ones are issued.

Producing authority, which is the instruction concerning when and how many products to make, relates only to a specific lot or quantity of products.

It is unique and covers no other products than those specified.

The original source of producing authority is usually the sales department, sometimes the production control department. Some special orders may come from other departments.

Producing authority may come to the control department in the form of:

Sales orders

Manufacturing requisitions

Master schedules and

Production programme releases.

The sales order itself, including the customer's specifications, is a producing authority when released to the production control department.

Manufacturing requisitions come to production control from finished stock department, where inventory record cards are kept up to date for all items carried in finished stock.

The established order points will determine the issuing of requisitions. Manufacturing requisitions are usually simple in forms often just the name and the identification number.

Master schedules (referred to as the over-all shedules of what the plant is to produce over an extended period in the future), as received by production control is an authority to produce.

Master schedules are issued periodically, covering three to six months' time, and usually small quantities of a great variety of products taking rather long time to make is scheduled. They are based on information regarding stock on hand, orders on hand, sales trends and prospects, and are usually used in irregular production.

Production programme releases is a producing authority covering but a few weeks' time. Usually they cover a few varieties of parts that can be made in less than two weeks, and every successive release contains all items with only minor adjustments in the quantities.

Almost all production is for stock.

There is no variation in products.

2. The Role of PPC in the Authorisation Procedure

Production planning and control receives the different types of authorisations from the various sources. The form of authorisation is usually changed and often expanded.

PPC translates the orders for finished products into several other orders to do the particular operations in the factory.

It releases to the factory these orders, which are both information and authority to manufacture.

For all practical purposes this information and authority is literally orders to produce, although the planning function formally is considered staff and hence advisory.

3. The Producing Authority in Different Types of Production

Type of Production	*Source of Authority*	*Type of Authority*
Single project	Sales dept.	Sales order
Intermittent		
To sales order	Sales dept.	Sales order
To stock		(Master schedule
Assembled products	Sales dept.	or
		(Prod. Programme Release
Parts	Production	Manufacturing
Continuous (To Stock)		
Assembled products	Sale dept.	Production programme release
Parts for assembly	Sales dept.	Production programme release
Non-assembled products	Sales dept.	Production programme release

ORDER CONTROL

Basic Information Required

Companies producing limited quantities of a wide variety of goods (job-lot shops) have the most complex problems of production control. In order control all authorisations, information, instructions, progress reports, etc., are prepared separately for each order and identified by the order number assigned to it.

Before instructions for the plant can be drawn up, the production control department needs comprehensive information about each new order and must have an extensive permanent file of information about materials, machines, operations, produtive capacity, and the like. Much of this information comes from past experience and is not written in all instances. For repeat orders most of the needed information can be obtained from past order files. Specific information needed:

1. Production Authorisation

Describes the products and the quantities wanted, completion dates and order number.

It is single one-time directive, applies only to the specific order.

After completion, the order is filed.

2. Bills of Material

Are of two kinds:

Master Bill of Material
Order Bill of Material

A mas r bill of materials for a product shows:

Name of the complete product and its identification number.

Component parts, identified by name and number.

Quantity of each part needed to make one complete product.

Source of parts, drawing numbers, casting number and pattern numbers may also be listed.

The master bill is made out by the engineering department and filed permanently in the production control department. It is made up in such form that duplicate copies can be made readily. The master itself is never used as an order to produce.

An order bill of materials is an order to produce a certain number of a product. It is a copy of the master bill, showing:

The qnantity of each part necessary to make the number of finished products called for on the order.

Availability of parts.

It is almost always necessary to prepare numerous copies of order bills since they are needed in several departments.

3. Blueprints and Specifications

Processing authorisation in the form of blueprints and specifications is issued by the engineering department. Blueprints show dimensions, tolerances, shapes and contours which the product is to have. Specifications include in text form additional information, such as:

Instructions on how to perform operations.

Required tests.

Statements that cannot be shown by a drawing.

Blueprints and specifications are often descriptions of the changes to be made in the product rather than specifications of the processes themselves.

4. Allowance for Scrap

Production control should know the expected loss rate on all operations. There are few on which products are not occasionally spoiled. Almost never, even after single operations, will all the items pass inspection. Some will have to be thrown out, others will require reworking, still others may be classified as seconds to be sold at reduced prices. Whenever possible, the proportion of good to spoiled items should be known so that accurate allowances for scrap can be made. On large special production such as ships, bridges, etc., no allowance for scrap is made because it is too expensive. Should a part be rejected in process, it must be repaired or replaced.

5. Operation Lists

Operation lists including all the operations the different products pass through, should always be on file in the production control department.

Every part must have its operation list. In its usual form it shows:

The name of the item.

The drawing number.

The identification code number,

The name and identification number of the product of which it is a part.

The size and kind of material from which it is made.

The amount of raw material needed to make up one unit.

The name and operation number of each operation required to process the part.

The sequence of operations.

The department in which each operation is performed.

The type of machine used for each operation.

All the information mentioned above is received from the engineering department and is a part of the routing procedure.

6. Machines Available

It is rather obvious that the production control department must have a record of all machines and equipment in the manufacturing departments. Although in many cases the machines and equipment are well known to the control people, a written list is preferable. In decentralised control this might not be necessary.

7. Operation Times

In order to plan the movement of work, the length of time for each operation must be known by the the production control department. This is especially true in centralised control. It is a great advantage to have a time standard department which can furnish this information.

8. Set Up Time and Idle Machine Time

Machine set up time (also includes tear down time) is usually an item of considerable importance and needs to be considered in planning the expected output from machines. In some places this time is included in the standard time for the particular operation, but in the cases where the set up time is more than one hour, it is a separate standard. Different kinds of set ups will take different amounts of time, and the production control department needs to have a record of each kind set up.

Expected idle machine time from other causes should also be known from past experience (knowledge of the expected).

Knowledge of the expected losses of machine time is necessary before the remaining time actually available for operations can be computed by the production control department. Scheduling cannot be done properly without these data.

Progress Information

All the information from 1 to 8 has dealt with the "planning ahead" part of production control. Much of the work of controlling production, however, is replanning rather than original planning. After orders are started in production, all of them very seldom move along according to schedule. It is therefore highly desirable for the production control department to get progress reports in order to replan and reschedule the remaining operations for orders which are not up to schedule.

In decentralised control, weekly reports from the foreman in each department are sent to production control. Some companies include in these reports reasons why orders are held up. There are also some that use "stock chasers", or "expediters" who find materials, eliminate reasons for delays and push selected orders through the plant.

The figure on the next page gives a preview of order control. Notice all the departments listed across the top, and all the steps you go through in order control listed down along the side. Notice, too, the arrows connecting the steps in the right-hand columns. Every step means papers (instructions and reports) going from one department to another.

Steps in a Typical Order Control Procedure

Description	*Customer*	*Sales Engineering Office*	*Stock Records*	*Route Clerk Preparation Forms*	*Schedule-Dispatch*	*Shop Foreman*	*Inspection-Shipping*	*Invoice Accounting Department*	*Cost Dept.*
1. Order placed.	1								
2. Plans, bill of material, and shop order prepared.		2							
3. Copy bill of material filed.		3							
4. Copy bill of material checked with stock records.			4						
5. Order routed; time cards, stores requisitions, duplicate order prepared.				5					
6. Copies of shop orders distributed to departments concerned.		6		6		6	6	6	6
7. Order shipping date entered on shop schedule.				7					
8. Material requisition sent out, material delivered to first process, rep. returned to planning department.		8				8			

9. On return of requisition, time card for first operation scheduled.		8				
10. Worker does operation, material delivered to next time card schedule.		9				
11. Process repeated until job is finished, inspcted and delivered to shipping.		10	10			
12. Good checked with shipping dept. copy of bill of material.		11		11		
13. Send bill of material to accounting dept., invoice prepared.				12		
14. Shipment and invoice to customer.	14				13	
15. Cost department compiles cost of job from time cards and material requisitions.						15

2

Materials Buying and Order Control

Materials and Parts Requirements

The type of materials to be used in production is generally determined by the engineering department because it has the necessary knowledge and equipment to check the physical characteristics necessary. Production control should also keep informed of new materials and new usages of existing materials in order to be able to evaluate the cost of using different types. The price of two alternative types may be the same and the phyisical characteristics equal, but the use of one may reduce the scrap compared to the other. In making an over-all comparison, production control can help the engineering department because it knows how much is needed.

Making or Buying Parts

This is usually a decision that has to be made by top management. The policy adopted depends upon how highly integrated and diversified the company chooses to become within the limits of its available capital and the volume of present and prospective business.

Advantages of Making

Delivery on time in the right quantity and quality.

Cost consideration loss inventory.

Special consideration such as lack of currency if buying from abroad.

Emergency cases.

Buying

Less investment in machines and equipment.

Simpler to manage is smaller or less diversified companies.

Price tends to be lower.

Sometimes it is advantageous to make most of the parts but to buy a few outside. Management does not have, however, to make the decision once and for all since it is almost always possible to buy equipment and go into making the parts formerly bought, or to close certain departments, sell the equipment and start to buy parts.

Requisitions for Finished Parts

Finished parts needed are issued from the finished parts stock room only in exchange for properly drawn up requisitions, which are prepared ahead of time as part of production control work. A list, which is usaually a copy of the order bill of materils, shows all the finished parts required to make up assembled, products. It serves as a requisition in contrast to requisitions for raw materials, which are usually separate, one for each kind material needed.

The items on the list may be with drawn immediately from stock and taken to an accumulation bin in the assembly department, or they may be reserved for the order on the stock record card and issued later. If any items on the list are not in stock, they may be made or bought. The order for making or requisition for buying should show the assemble order number for which they are being obtained.

Requisitions for Raw Materials

Raw materials are generally issued for use in the manufacture of parts. These parts are manufactured on separate individual productiion orders. Raw materials requisitions are in most cases individual requisitions in the form of small slips of paper or cards which in many cases are made to fit mechanical tabulation equipment. Fig. 2.1 shows an example of such a card.

The source of information for calculating the quantity of raw materials needed is the route sheet, while for finished parts it is the bill of materials.

Raw materials requisitions are usually made out by PPC department well in advance of production. They are generally held there until a short time before the materials are needed and are then released directly to the stock room for filling. Often raw materials are received into the stock room measured in terms of one unit and are issued from it in terms of another.

For minor items such as washers, nuts, bolts, nails, tacks or rivets, no requisitions are made out because the figuring of the need for each order plus the issuing of a requisition will cost more than the use of the items.

Machines and Machine Time

Because the assembly operation from production control point of view is considered as one operation. the big job for the department is the production of parts. Schedules for manufacturing departments are dependent on the machine requirements of the orders. It is necessary to know what machines are needed and how much time is required for each in order to plain for operations, The information needed is available from previous

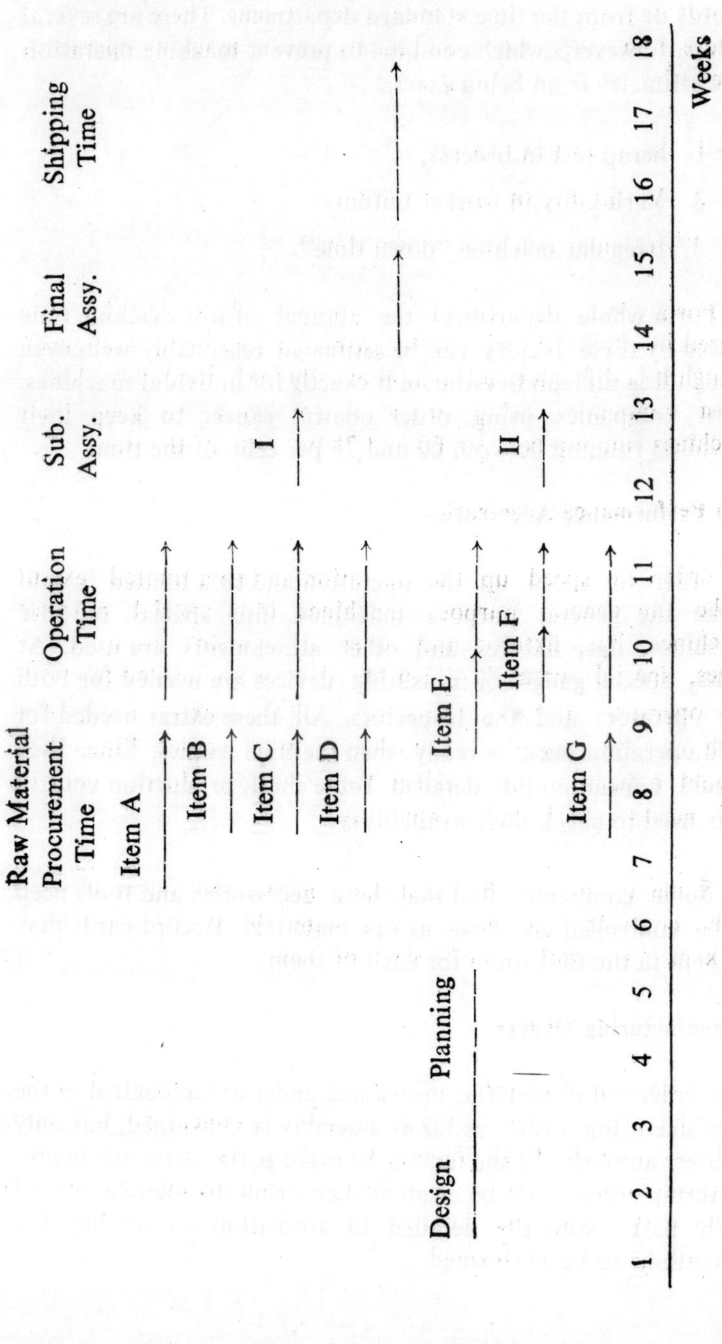

Fig. 2.1: Diagramatic Plan for Arranging a Schedule

records or from the time standard department. There are several factors, however, which combine to prevent machine operation time estimates from being exact:

1. Scrap lost in process.
2. Variability in worker output.
3. Irregular machine "down time".

For a whole department the amount of lost machine time caused by these factors can be estimated reasonably well, even though it is difficult to estimate it exactly for individul machines. Most companies using order control expect to keep their machines running between 60 and 75 per cent of the time.

Job Performance Accessories

In order to speed up the operation and to a limited extent make the general purpose machines into special purpose machines, jigs, fixtures and other attachments are used. At times, special gauges or measuridg devices are needed for both the operators and the inspectors. All these extras needed for each operation must be ready when the time comes, Since they should appear on the detailed route sheet, production control only need to check their availability.

Some companies find that these accessories and tools need to be controlled as close as raw materials. Record cards may be kept in the tool room for each of them.

Manufacturing Orders

The order bill of material mentioned under order control is the manufacturing order as far as assembly is concerned, but only indirect authority to the factory to make parts. Separate manufacturing orders must be originated covering the manufacture of each part. Note the detailed in formation concerning the operations to be performed.

The information needed is obtained by production control from master route sheet or "variable" masters. Companies making fairly simple single piece products, put the drawing of the part on the same piece of paper with the order itself.

Companies using the manufacturing order with rather detailed information, make up numerous copies of the order, one for every department concerned. Those which do not use the manufacturing (or shop) order to authorise production, use individual job tickets which cover only one operation. They are made out ahead by the production control department and way held until the worker is ready to start the job.

Move Orders

Movements of materials in intermittent industries are made by hand truck or power truck rather than by conveyor. The truckers need directives to tell them what materials to move and where to move. Copy of the ticket it turned to PPC department after the material has been moved. Some companies use two-radio to direct truckers.

Material Identification Tags

As a general rule, material in process in intermittent manufacturing is not self-identifying, and needs to have some sort of identification so that it will be used in the order for which it is intended. The method need is to write both the order number and a very short word description such as "back plate" or "left bracket holder" on a small ticket. The identification is generally attached to the container in which the material or the item is transported and stored.

Other Forms

There are several other forms used in connection with the preparation for production:

Defective parts report.

Machine loads (will be discussed later).

Request for change (will be discussed later).

Schedule sheet (will be discussed later).

Scrap report, and other reports,

SCHEDULING IN ORDER CONTROL

Scheduling sets the time when the work is to be done. It has been defined as the process of fitting jobs into a logical timetable. The most familiar example of scheduling is the planning of the movement of the various classes and types of trains on a modern railroad. All the different trains must be scheduled accurately to avoid accidents and costly train delays and at the same time to utilise the tracks and equipment.

Scheduling in order control means the planning of the different orders through the different machines to avoid collisions and delays and at the same time utilise the facilities. It deals both with orders and machines. Many manufacturing orders are in process at all times, and it is necessary to indicate which orders should be processed ahead of others and when each should be completed. Processing is generally machine operations so scheduling is also concerned with sequences of jobs on machines, and with the times when the machine is to be used for each job.

Schedules must be flexible in order to meet changes resulting from workers, materials or machines, and to allow for rush orders.

Order Scheduling

Most customer orders have definite dates for delivery. The same is true for items on shortage lists of parts for lots of assembled products. The wanted date is a rough schedule for an order. The date when the first operation should start can be estimated by working backwards, allowing some time for each operation. In addition to operation time plus move time, the fact that machines and men cannot wait for a particular lot must be included.

Fig. 2.1 shows a theoretical diagram fro arranging a schedule. The various portions of the entire job are shown as they progress from left to right. Note the differences in procurement time and operation time for the assembly. In this example all the items for the two subassemblies needed some procurement time. For subassembly I, the operation time for the items is identical while it varies for the items in subassembly II. In other cases most of the raw materials needed for the items may be in stock, the operation time vary from item to item, one subassembly may be finished before the other, and so on. There are, of course, numerous variations in design time procurement time, operation time, subassembly time and assembly time. For the production control department it is helpful to set up a rough schedule plan for each order.

Machine Scheduling

Machine scheduling is concerned with apportioning the available machine time to orders in accordance with order schedule requirements. Since actual machine time often varies considerably from anticipated. most companies do not plan the exact use of individual machines hour by hour for days ahead if they are to be used for several orders. Machine scheduling is more a matter of determining the sequence of jobs to be done on each machine than it is a matter of machine time schedules.

At simple method used by some companies calls for the producing departments to do the scheduling on the basis of the wanted completion date. Wanted dates for each operation are not shown on the shop orders, but the wanted completion date is shown. The foreman gets a copy of the shop orders ahead of time to plan the work in his own department.

A more common method is to establish wanted dated for every operation and then require the foremen to use them as their guides.

A third method is to use individual operation wanted dates but with shop orders held by production control rather than the foreman. A dispatch clerk employed in the production control department has an office in the producing department and assigns orders on the basis of operation wanted dates.

Machine scheduling is usually carried out without written schedules of machine use. Instead the shop orders or the job tickets are filed for each machine separately in order according to wanted dates. Various types of boards (described in a later lecture) are used for this purpose. All these systems are very flexible, since a schedule change is only a matter of changing the placement of one or more of the order sheets from one file location to another.

Control of Assembly

Although the control of assembly is simpler than control of parts, faulty production control at this stage has more serious consequences than in the production of parts. On the assembly floor it is essential that all parts be ready for assembly, that special tools be available as well as work area and men. Following is a list of some of the typical characteristics of assembly control.

1. Confirm that all parts and special accessory apparatus are ready.
2. Authority to proceed with assembly is conveyed in the copy of the order bill of material sent to the assembly department.
3. Assembly generally extends over a period of time during which products are finished one by one until the order is completed.

4. The assembly of finished products ordinarily is carried on without specific move orders to truckers or material handlers.

5. Instructions to the assemblers are confined to verbal instructions from the foreman.

6. Usually parts of assembled products must be put together in a certain order which is determined ahead by the engineering department.

7. If the order is for a very complex product and only one is ordered, the progress of assembly work must be estimated from time to time so it can be compared to the expected progress.

Machine Loading

Machine load may be defined as the number of hours of work assigned to each machine or group of similar machines beyond the current date. Each new job assigned to a machine increases the future load factor, and each finished job reduces the load already assigned. In the cases where the machines are used for the same product, the load can be expressed in terms of the product.

The load factor is estimated from a route sheet or accurately determined from an operation sheet which may have all the operations time studied. In addition, machine loads have to include the set-up or preparation time for each machine when a a job is changed.

Objectives of Machine Loading

1. To provide an accurate method of showing the backlog of work in the plant.

2. To show the unbalanced conditions in different portions of tne plant.

3. Maintain full utilisation or all the machines and keep down time to a minimum.

Effect of Overload

A single-shift forty-hour week has only forty hours capacity available from each machine. If more work is assigned than there are hours in the normal period several courses of action are possible.

(a) Some of the load can be shifted to other machines of the same type or machines that can do the work.

(b) Overtime may be used.

(c) Two or three shifts may be introduced.

(d) New methods may be introduced.

(e) Improved scheduling.

(f) Subcontracting the bottlenecks and excess loads.

(g) Buying additional machines.

Effect of Underload

The underloading of a machine may be caused by one of several factors. Some are serious; others are temporary and can be easily corrected.

(a) Buying expensive machines which produce more than can be used and thereby underload the machine.

(b) Some job-order shops may underload because of fast service to their customers. This may be avoided by developing standard products.

(c) When certain machines are underloaded, the sales department might be able to increase the sales of certain products.

(d) Improve scheduling to avoid underloading.

(f) Reduce working hours or sell machines.

To keep a visual record of the loads on machines and departments, many companies use different forms of charts.

The Gantt Chart

This chart was developed during World War I by Henry L. Cantt, one of the pioneers in scientific management. The feature of the chart is that work planned and work done are shown in the same space in their relation to each other and in their relation to time.

The symbols used in the chart include:

1. An angle (˥) opening to the right, indicating the date or hour when work is to begin.
2. An angle (>) opening to the left, indicating the date on which work is to be completed.
3. A figure (| 10 |) placed at the left side of a space indicating the amount of work scheduled for any period of time.
4. A figure (| 49) placed at the right side of a space indicating the amount of work done up to any specified time.

Work done during any period of time is represented by light lines. Heavy lines show the cumulative amount of work done and its relation to the amount scheduled to be done up to any given date.

A Gantt chart shows only work which is to be done in distinction to progress charts which has been done.

Merits of Gantt Charts

Advantages:

1. Prospective bottlenecks may be detected before they occur.

2. They show up production delays immediately.

3. The help in planning production.

4. They are most valuable when production is running near capacity level.

5. Customer promise dates can more certainly be met.

Drawbacks:

1. Charts are relatively static.
2. They are not well adopted to show changes which occur all the time.

ROUTING PROCEDURE IN ORDER CONTROL

Routing is the determination of how the product is going to be made. In its broad sense the procedure involves plotting the path to be followed through the plant, office, warehouse, or store.

In order control it means to decide in detail the methods, machines and sequence of operations each product or part should follow. For all new parts or products the routing is carried out by the engineering department. Route sheets are filed, however, by the production control department to be issued on repeat orders. Only when changes in product design occur, the engineering department is contacted.

The figure on the next page shows a route sheet.

The elements of routing in their natural sequence, are as follows:

1. Analysis of the product to determine the possible ways or methods of making it, depending on:

(a) Machines available.

(b) Materials available.

(c) Cost consideration.

2. Study of the various methods to determine the "one best way" under existing circumstances.

3. Assembling of complete data on available machines, equipment and tools useful for the job, to determine their capacity and plan for requirements to establish balanced production.

4. Determining on the basis of methods adopted, what type or kind of special equipment (jigs, fixtures), or machines can be used to advantage, and whether the advantage justifies their construction or purchase.

5. Deciding on machine speeds and feeds for the purpose of establishing maximum productivity and operation times.

6. Figuring operation time standards for the purpose of balancing production, or other activities, through proper routing. Overall production time includes machine set-up, average machine downtime, inspection and material handling.

7. Determining the sequence or route of operation.

8. Route sheets must be broken down into subassemblies so that all components will be available for synchronising with the main assembly.

9. Preparing work sheets for carrying out the routing details.

10. Working out plans so that routing fits into the operations of centralised or decentralised control procedures already established.

Interdepartmental Route Sheet

Routing Sheet

Part Name........................ Material......................

Part No. .... Quantity.........................

Order No. .... Issue Date.......................

Route No......................... Complete By...................

Operation Number	Dept. No.	Operation	Machine Number	Tools	Standard Time	Price

When an item can be completed within a department, it is customary for the supervisor to plan and route the job. Where several departments are involved, central routing is advisable.

The operations list discussed in the previous period is somewhat similar to the route sheets, but does not include so much detailed information.

3

Material Requirements Planning

P. G. BURCHER

1. Introduction

In contrast to the classical inventory control approach to the planning and control of materials, the technique, known as material requirements planning (MRT), looks at a future requirement for the finished product in terms of a master production schedule and uses this and other information to generate the requirements for all the sub-assemblies, components and raw materials which go to make up the finished product.

This technique has, in essence, been used under different names for many years, particularly for the purchase of special materials in the jobbing industries, that is, the time-phasing of material ordering. However, the advent of low cost computing has brought the term material requirements planning to the fore in the planning and control of the manufacture of multi-component assemblies. In fact, MRP forms the central module of the majority of commercially available production control software packages.

As has been mentioned, MRP is concerned with the manufacture of multi-component assemblies and relies on the fact that the demands for all sub-assemblies, components and raw materials are dependent upon the demand for the finished product itself. They are said to have 'dependent demands'.

There are also some items which have 'independent demands' that is, the demand for them does not depend on the demand for any other item. Notably, the finished product itself usually has an independent demand in that it depends solely on the customer purchasing the product. Components and sub-assemblies may also have independent demands in the form of spare parts sales requirements.

It is interesting to note that in a recent survey, 92% of enginesring companies produced assembled products, that is to say, they had to deal with a proportion of dependent demand items.

Independent demand items may be satisfactorily controlled using the classical inventory control approach, for example, the reorder level policy. However, for dependent demand items, MRP offers considerable advantages in ensuring that all the parts for the assembly of the product are available at the right time. It also reduces overall stockholding costs whilst improving the service that the stock is providing.

To illustrate this point a simple is shown in figure 3.1.

This example shows that a saving in stock holding costs is one of the objectives of an MRP system.

In order to carry out its calculations, the MRP package requires three tppes of information to be supplied, namely:

(i) The master production schedule for the finished product;

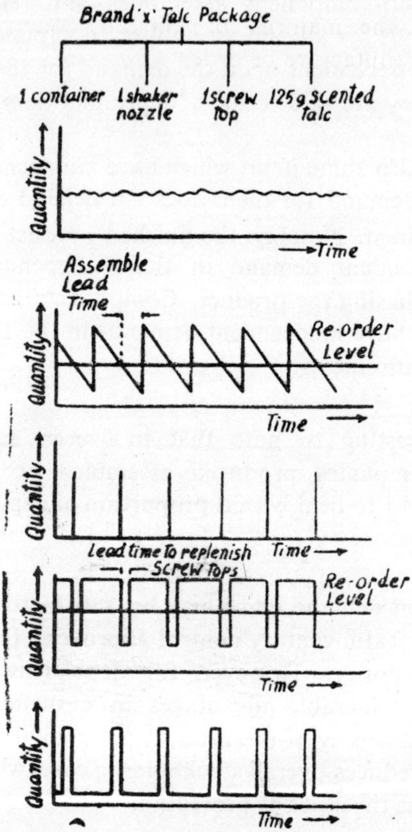

Fig. 3.1: A Comparison of the Behaviour of Component Stocks using a Re-order Level Policy and MRP

(ii) The bill of material which contains details of which raw materials, components and sub-assemblies go to make up the finished products; and

(iii) Information concerning the status of all materials held in inventory.

Having performed its calculations, the package then produces reports, the majority of which are concerned with what and when to manufacture or order.

This system is shown in general outline in figure 3.2.

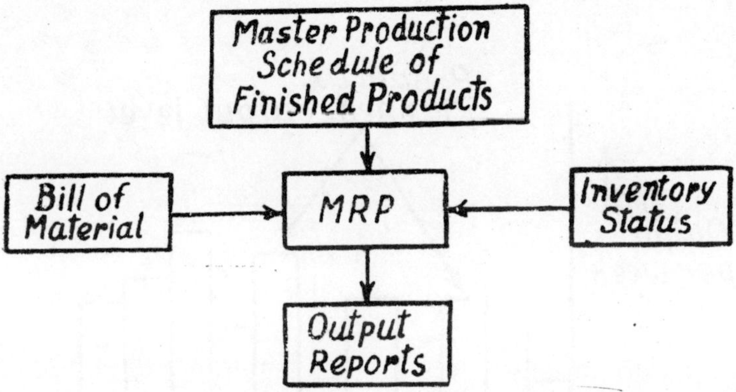

Fig. 3.2 General MRP System Outline

2. Elements of the MRP System

The total MRP System (figure 3.2) consists of several elements: the inputs, the package itself which carries out the calculations and the output reports. Each element may vary in its exact description, depending on the company and product in any particular case, but it is important to understand the purpose of the element and the various choices which are available.

3. The Master Production Schedule

The master production schedule is a management commitment to produce certain volumes of finished products in particular time periods in the future and should not be confused with the term 'sales forecast'.

A master schedule is created for each finished product using known customer orders, sales forecasts and a knowledge of the manufacturing capacity. It is likely that the schedule will contain a major proportion of firm customer orders in the most immediate time periods and mostly forecasts in the later periods of the planning horizon (see figure 3.3).

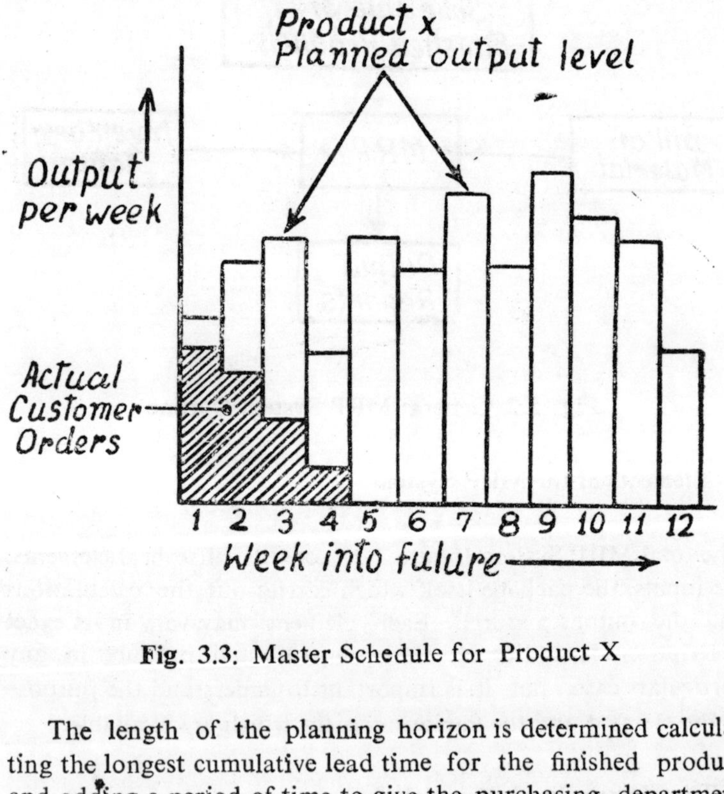

Fig. 3.3: Master Schedule for Product X

The length of the planning horizon is determined calculating the longest cumulative lead time for the finished product and adding a period of time to give the purchasing department visibility over future requirements, so that they are able to take advantage of bulk purchasing discounts. The longest cumulative lead time is the sum of all the lead times along the longest route from placing an order for a raw material to completing the finished product (see figure 3.4).

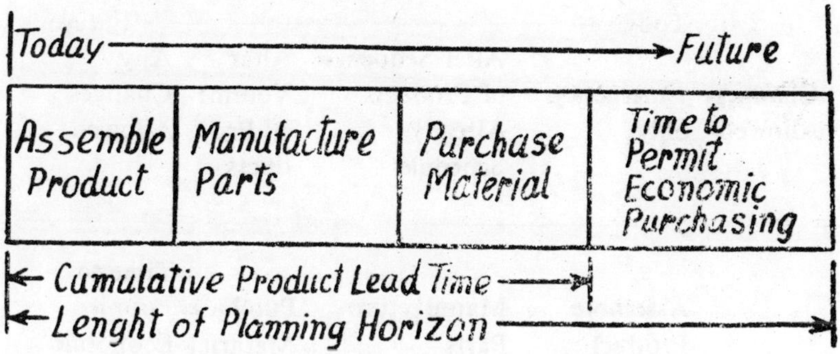

Fig. 3.4: Master Schedule Planning Horizon

For many companies in practice this will entail using planning horizons of between a year and eighteen months. Since the further ahead a forecast is made, the less accurate it is likely to be, it would be unrealistic to expect that no changes would be allowed to the master schedule, particularly in its later stages. There are however, increasing difficulties in making changes to the schedule the closer that the beginning or 'front end' of the schedule is approached.

One method of controlling the changes to the master production schedule is to split the planning horizon into time zones, each of which has different constraints on the type of change which can be made (see figure 3.5).

Essentially, that period of the schedule which represents finished products which are currently being assembled should only be changed in emergency situations, since parts and subassemblies will have already been manufactured to the original schedule.

In that part of the planning horizon which represents parts currently being manufactured, it may be possible to alter the sequence of the finished products already scheduled, bear in mind material and capacity availabilities.

	Tody			→Future
Changes Allowed	Emergency only	Alter Sequence of Products Already Schedule	Alter Volume of Products	Any Changes Allowed
	Assemble Product	Manufacture Parts	Purchase Matarial	Time to Permit Economic Purchasing

Fig 3.5: Changes Allowed to the Master Schedule

In the period which represents orders for materials that have been placed on suppliers, it may be feasible to alter the quantities of finished products on the master schedule if it is possible to make the consequent alterations of material quantities on the open orders with suppliers.

In the last section of the planning horizon, or 'back-end' of the schedule, which represents forward information for the purchasing department, it should be possible to make alterations to both the sequence and volume of finished products scheduled, presuming of course, that checks have first been made with the purchasing department regarding any major bulk material purchases which may have been made on the basis of the original information.

Apart from the sales of finished products, a company might also be concerned with the supply of spares in the form of components or sub-assemblies. As described previously, these items have independent demands. However, these independent demands can be incorporated into a MRP system by adding them to the generated dependent demands for the items in the relevant time periods.

As with the master production schedule, the independent spare parts demands could be made up of firm customer orders and sales forecasts as in figure 3.6.

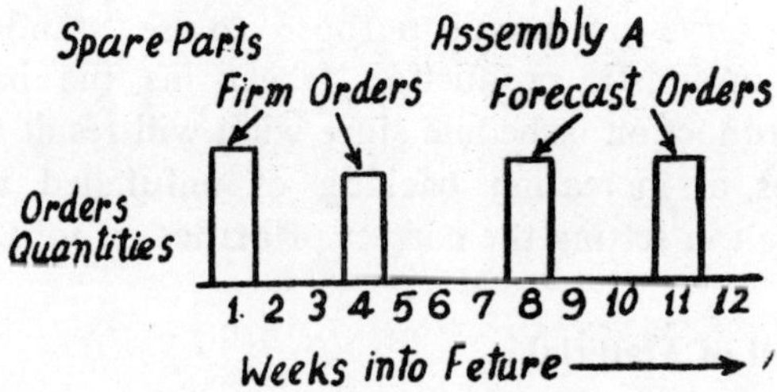

Fig. 3.6: Spares Demand for Assembly A

The time periods used in the master schedule will be a result of the degree of control required in the overall production planning and control system and for most companies it is accepted that time periods in excess of one week do not give sufficient control for the setting of priorities for manufactured components and their subsequent progressing.

Some companies have tackled the problem of the choice of time period or time 'bucker'by adopting variable lenth periods, as in figure 3.7, which give the possibility of greater control of the final assembly operations and less detailed control for the bulk purchasing of materials.

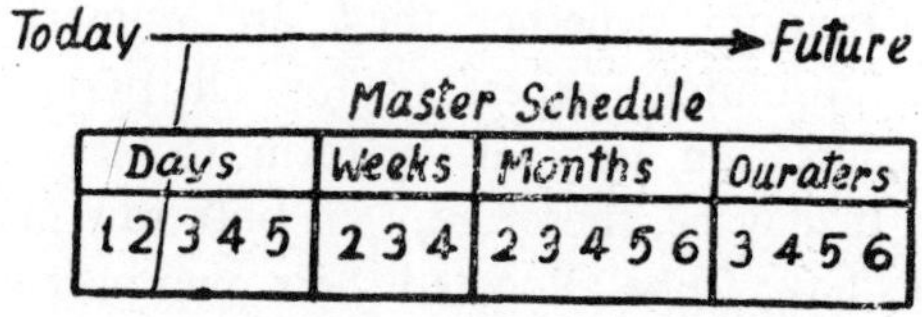

Fig. 3.7: Master Schedule with Variable Length Time Periods

The master production schedule should be, above all, a realistic picture of what can be achieved, based on past experience.

It will serve no useful purpose to use 'standard' rates of output or optimistic production targets as the basis for the master production schedule since what will result are excessive inventories, an increasing backlog of unfulfilled requirements and difficult in setting the correct priorities on jobs.

4. The Bill of Material

The bill of material (BOM) is a file or set of files which basically contain the 'recipe' for each finished product. The 'racipe' in a manufactured goods environment consists of information regarding which materials, components and sub-assemblies go together to make up each finished product, held on what is often known as a Product Structure file; and all the standard information about each item, such a part number, description, unit of measure, lead time for manufacturing or procurement etc., held on what is often known as a Part Master file.

For each finished product a bill of material is originally created from the design and production engineering information. This information will initially be in the form of drawings (see Fig 3.8) and assembly charts (see Fig. 3.9) which together with information on the relevant lead times form the basis of the inputs to the BOM.

Whilst most MRP systems can cope with part numbers allocated at random, whether they are numeric or alphanumeric, it is absolutely necessary for all parts or material within the organisation, in whatever form, to be given a unique part number. It may be, therefore, that bulk raw materials and sub-assemblies have to be allocated their own part numbers for the first time, if an MRP system is to be implemented.

It may appear obvious that the information on the BOM needs to be accurate, since inaccuracies can lead to incorrect

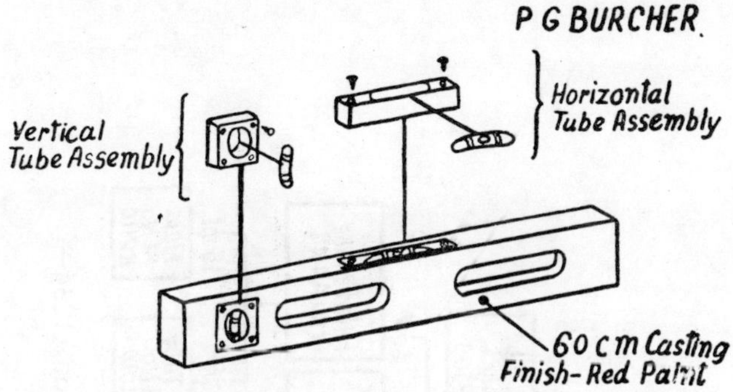

Fig. 8: Design Drawing (simplified) of Part No. A1234—a 60 cm. Spirit Level

items or incorrect quantities of items being ordered. However, the problem of file accuracy is complicated by the fact that in many operating environments there are continual changes to the BOM in the form of product modifications. These modifications may originate from many sources, for example: safety legislation, production process changes, improvements for marketing purposes, value analysis exercises, etc.

The control of the implementation of modifications can be a very time-consuming task for some companies, especially since factors such as the depletion of un-modified stocks and the timing of combined modifications have also to be considered

One other piece of information that has to be recorded on the BOM is the assembly level at which the item occurs in the product structure. There is an almost universally accepted level numbering system which allocates level 0 to the finished product and increases the level number as the raw material stage is approached, for example see figure 3.10.

The number of levels of assembly breakdown is determined by the complexity of the product and can be as high as twelve for products as complex as aircraft engines.

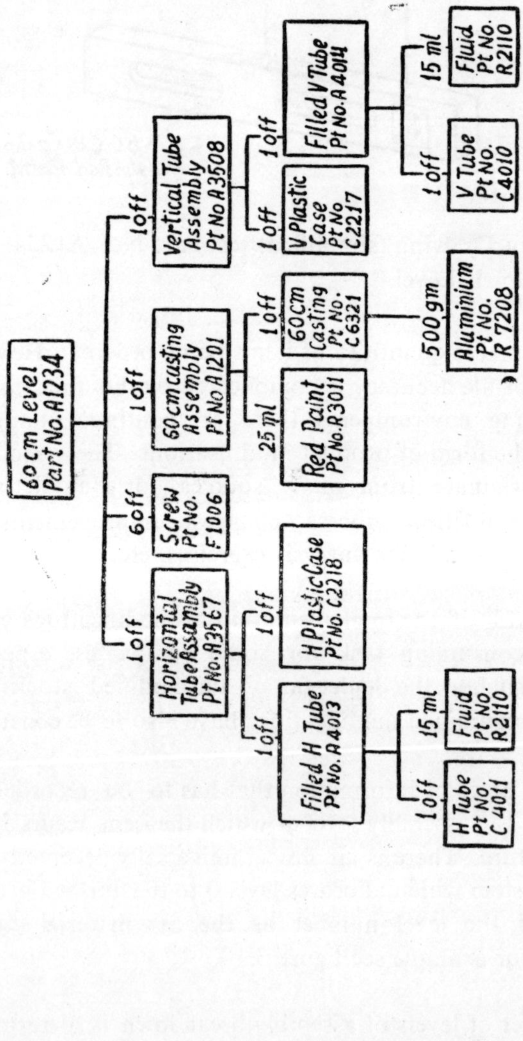

Fig. 3.9: Assembly Chart (simplified) for Part No. A1234—a 60 cm. Spirit Level

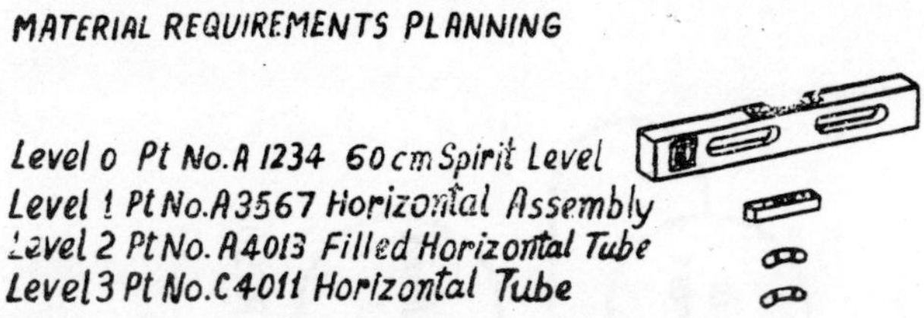

Fig. 3.10: Parts Structure and Assembly Level Numbering

The key characteristic of a bill of material should be its accuracy, since 'one can never produce mince pies on time using the recipe for sausage rolls !'

5. Inventory Status File

The inventory status file keeps a record of all transactions and balances of all stock throughout the organisation. The transactions are mainly receipts and issues, starting with the 'On Order' condition and eventually finishing with the issue of the completed product out of the factory. Other transations may record occurrences such as inspection rejects or stock adjustments as a result of physical stock checks.

Many organisations use the concept of the 'stock condition' to describe the stage which the material has reached, for example: 500 kgs of aluminium part no. R 7208 has been inspected and is in the raw material store ready for issue into Work in Progress. An example of a possible stock condition route is shown in figure 3.11.

If a greater degree of control is required, the work in progress stock condition may itself be split into a number of separate stock conditions, so that a batch of items may be monitored from one operation to the next (see figure 3.12).

It should be noted that as material progress from one stock condition to the next, its part number may also change. For

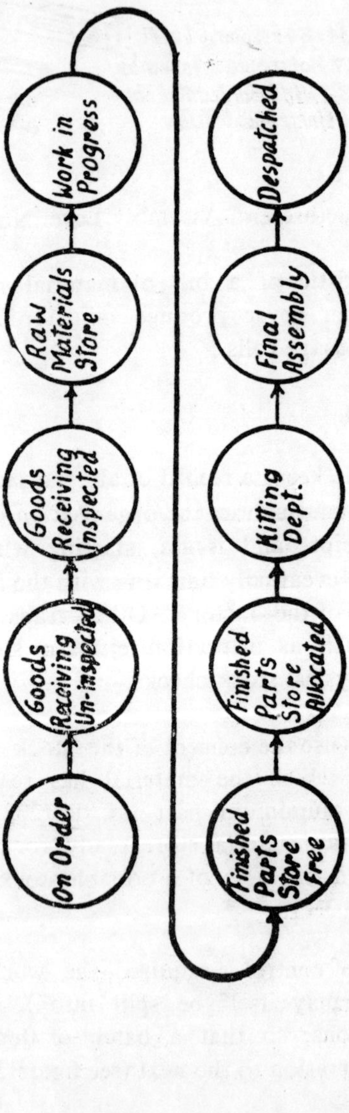

Fig. 3.11: Stock Condition Route for Aluminium Part No. R7208

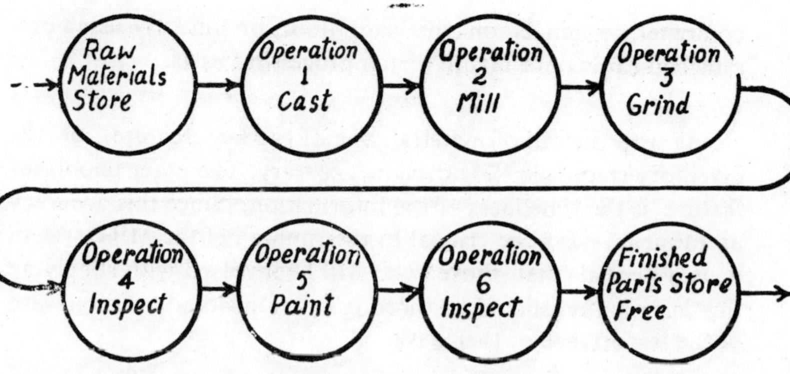

Fig. 3.12: Work in Progress Stock Conditions

example, when 6 screws (Part No. F1006) become part of the spirit level final assembly (Part No. A1234), the balance of Part No. F1006 (screws) in the 'kitting' condition is reduced by 6 and the balance of Part No. A1234 (assembly) in the 'final assembly' condition is increased by 1.

The actual method that is used to input the inventory transactions to the inventory status file may vary considerably. At one extreme, the information may be input on a batch processing basis using punched cards that have been punched from handwritten information.

In the early days of MRP, this method of updating with weekly or bi-weekly processing runs was most common, Unfortunately this led to considerable problems because of the untimeliness of the information.

At the other extreme, it is now possible to have automatic monitoring devices of work centres which feed numbers of items completed directly into the computer file.

Most MRP users are currently using either direct 'on-line' inventory updating prehaps using pre-punched cards through computer terminals on the shop-floor, or similarly using pre-punched cards on a nightly batch processing basis.

As with the bill of material, one of the key features of the inventory status file should be its accurary. The other important feature is the timeliness of the information. Since this accuracy and timeliness will be critical to the running of the MRP system it is essential that those who will be involved with supplying this information should be thoroughly trained and made aware of the importance of their task.

6. The MRP Package

The MRP package carries out calculations on a level by level basis which convert the master schedule of finished products into suggested orders for all the sub-assemblies, components and raw materials. These calculations or 'requirements generation runs' are likely to be carried out on the computer every one or two weeks so that the situation is kept constantly up-to-date.

At each level of assembly breakdown, the package undertakes three steps in its calculations before continuing to the next lower level. These steps are as follows:

(i) It generates gross requirements for the item by 'exploding' the 'planned start' quantities of the next higher level assembly, by reference to the bill of material structure file.

e.g.,

A 'planned start' of 200 spirit levels (Pt. No. A1234 in week 15 would be exploded to give gross requirements of 1200 screws (Pt. No. F1006) in week 15. (Refer to figure 3.9 for an assembly chart).

(ii) The gross requirements are amended by the amount of inventory of that item that is expected to be available in each week *i.e.*, on hand plus scheduled receipts. This information is obtained from the inventory status file and the amended requirements are called the net requirements.

e.g.,

In week 15 a total of 800 screws are expected to be available, so the gross requirement of 1200 is amended to give a net requirement of 400 screws in week 15.

(iii) The net requirements are then offset by the relevant lead time for the item to give planned starts for initiating the manufacture or purchase of the item.

e.g.,

If the lead time for the screws (Pt. No. F1006) is 4 weeks, the net requirements of 400 screws in week 15 are offset as follows:

Week No.	11	12	13	14	15	16
Net Requirements					400	
Planned Starts	400					

To summarise, in its simplest form, the MRP package would calculate the requirement of screws for each period of the planning horizon as in figure 3.13.

The calculation ahead assumes that the only use of the screw (Part No. F1006) is in the assembly of the 60cm spirit level. If this were not the case and if its usage were common to other products assembled by the organisation, for example 40cm

Part No. A1234 *60 cm. Spirit Level Assembly*

	10	11	12	13	14	15	16
Week No.	10	11	12	13	14	15	16
(Master Schedule) Planned Starts	400	300	200	200	300	200	400

Part No. F1006 *Screw* *LT=4*

Week No.		10	11	12	13	14	15	16
Gross Requirements		2400	1800	1200	1200	1800	1200	2400
Scheduled Receipts			6000					
Projected Stock on hand	3200	800	5000	3800	2600	800	0	0
Net Requirements							400	2400
Planned Starts			400	2400				

Fig. 3.13: MRP Calculation Example

and 80cm spirit levels, then the gross requirements for the screw would have been the aggregated requirements generated from the planned starts of all the assemblies using that screw.

7. Batch Sizing in MRP Systems

The simplified approach to the calculation of requirements has, so far, assumed that the net requirements would be translated directly into planned starts, resulting in manufacturing component schedules and purchasing schedules which do not take any account of the cost of machine set-ups or the cost of ordering. In other words, marking the requirements as they occur on a week by week basis, otherwise known as the lot-for-lot policy,[2] will certainly reduce overall stockholding costs, but will increase costs incurred through excessive set-up and ordering costs for small batches.

To take account of the total costs of managing the materials, that is holding costs and ordering or set-up costs, batch sizing rules may need to be applied for the manufacturing or purchasing of items.

There are basically three different methods of batching requirements together; these are fixed quantitly batching rules, fixed period coverage batching rules and dynamic batching rules.

(*i*) *Fixed Quantity Batching Rules*

The fixed quantity rule essentially states that every time an item is manufactured or bought it is done so in batches of size '*X*' (or multiples of '*X*'). The size of the batch may be determined by a physical constraint of the manufacturing process *e.g.*, furnace size, by considering the quantity that would normally be produced in one shift or in one week, or by some 'economic' calculation.

The calculation that is most likely to be used for an economic fixed batch size is the so-called economic order quantity formula as used in the 'classical' re-order level policy (see page 290) *i.e.*,

$$EOQ = \sqrt{\frac{2A\ C_o}{iC_m}}$$

where A=Demand per time period: C_o=Set-up (or Ordering) Cost; and iC_m=Cost of holding one item for one period; (i being the holding interest rate and C_m the value of the item).

However, it should be noted that in an MRP system, the assumptions upon which the EOQ calculation is based are not valid, that is; a re-order level policy is not in operation and there is not continuous demand and a gradual depletion of stock of the item. Consequently, although the EOQ may be a guide to the 'best' batch size, it cannot be guaranteed that the implementation will result in minimising total inventory operating costs.

An example of the operation of a fixed quantity batching rule using the EOQ calculation is shown in figure 3.14.

Part No. C6321 *60cm Casting* *LT=1* *Batch Rule=Fixed Quantity*
Batch Size=700

Week No.	20	21	22	23	24	25	26	27	28	29
Net Requirements	0	350	100	0	400	0	200	50	100	300
Batched Requirements	—	700	—	—	700	—	—	—	—	700
Planned Starts	700	—	—	700	—	—	—	—	700	—

Fig. 3.14: Example of a Fixed Quantity Batching Rule

Note : If A, (average demand) = 150 per week

C_s, (set-up cost) = £500

Ci_m, (holding cost = £0.3.0 per item per week

$$\text{Then EOQ} = \sqrt{\frac{2\times150\times500}{0.3}} = 707$$

∴ Use Batch Size =700 items

(ii) Fixed Period Coverage Batching Rules

Fixed period coverage rules calculate a batch size by batching together the net requirements for the next '*y*' periods ahead. The coverage period may be chosen to fit in with a cycle scheduling[3] approach to stop loading where, for example, machined components may be manufactured on a three weekly repeated cycle with one third of components starting in week 1, one third in week 2 and so on. If the choice is not determined by this constraint, an 'economic' coverage period may be calculated by relating the economic order quantity calculation to an equivalent number of time periods' coverage.

An example of the operation of a fixed period coverage rule is shown in Fig. 3.15.

Part No. C6321 *60cm Casting* *LT=1* *Batch Rule=Fixed Period*
Period=5

Week No.	20	21	22	23	24	25	26	27	28	29
Net Requirements	0	350	100	0	400	0	200	50	100	300
Batched Requirements	—	850	—	—	—	—	650+	—	—	—
Planned Starts	850	—	—	—	—	650+	—	—	—	—

Fig. 3.15: Example of a Fixed Period Coverage Batching Rule

Note: Using the same information as in Fig. 3.14 the Fixed Period would be calculated as follows:

$$\frac{EOQ}{A}\text{(average weekly demand)}=\frac{700}{150}\simeq 5 \text{ weeks.}$$

(*iii*) *Dynamic Batching Rules*

With dynamic batching rules, the computer uses an algorithm which attempts to arrive at a batching schedule which minimises inventory operating costs. One example of a dynamic rules is the least total cost or part period algorithm.[2] This algorithm consists of computing the cumulative holding costs and stopping at the batch size just short of the point where cumulative holding costs exceed the set-up cost. It makes the cost comparison by first calculating the ratio of the set up cost (C_s) to to the holding cost (iC_m) known as the part period value (*PPV*) *i.e.*, how many parts may be held for how many periods whose holding cost will equate to the set up cost. For example, using the data in Fig. 3.14, the *PPV* would be 500/.3=1667 part periods.

The Part Period Algorithm would calculate the batches as follows:

PPV=1667

Week No.	*Net Reqts.*	*Cumulative Batch Size*	*Inventory Held*	*Number of Periods*	*Cumulative Part Periods*
21	350	350	0	0	0
22	100	450	100	1	100
23	0	450	0	2	100
24	400	850	400	3	1300
25	0	850	0	4	1300
26	200	1050	200	5	2300(>1667)

∴ 1st Batch of 850 required in week 21

(*Contd.*)

26	200	200	0	0	0
27	50	250	50	1	50
28	100	350	100	2	250
29	300	650	300	3	1150

Second batch of at least 650 required in week 26 (on the next MRP run the net requirement of Week 30 may be included in the batch).

In this particular example the part period algorithm has produced identical planned starts to those shown in Fig. 3.15 although, of course, this will not always be the case.

Each type of batching rule has its own advantages and disadvantages. The fixed quantity rule is easily understood and may fit in well with manufacturing process constraints or suppliers' standard order sizes. However, it suffers from the drawbacks of generating orders at irregular intervals and, compared to the other methods of batching, it generates higher stock levels.

Since the fixed period coverage rule is directly related to the future periods' requirements, it is more economical in terms of the overall stock levels generated and, as mentioned previously, it may fit in well with the balancing of the workload on the shopfloor. However, it may result in sizes of batches which fluctuate considerably especially if there are periods with zero net requirements.

Theoretically the dynamic batching rules, especially the part period algorithm, are superior to the other two methods of batch sizing in the reduction of costs. However, they suffer the disadvantages of not being understood as easily and of generating differing batch sizes at uncertain time intervals which, in turn, may lead to difficulties in shop loading.

In general, it should be noted that any batching that takes place at high levels in the assembly structure will affect the requirements for all the constituent items at the lower levels *i.e.*, requirements will be similarly bunched together and required earlier. Therefore, unless set-up or ordering costs are significantly high, it may be advantageous to generate planned starts on a lot-for-lot basis rather than batching, since this will certainly lead to lower holding costs and will keep the relative priorities on manufactured items realistic.

8. Setting Safety Stocks in MRP Systems

Safety stocks are held in any manufacturing system to cater for uncertainty. In an MRP system the major cause of uncertainty, that of the future usage of the item, has been mainly eliminated since items should be produced to meet a plan—the master schedule. Therefore, overall, safety stocks in an MRP system should be significantly lower than in a system using classical inventory control policies.

However, safety stocks are still needed because of uncertainties in supply both in terms of the variation of actual lead times and the variation of quantites supplied caused by inspection rejects and material shortages. There will also be changes of demand caused by short-term (emergency) changes to the master schedule and unexpected demands for items such as spares.

The statistical techniques of establishing safety stocks used in classical inventory control systems are mainly inappropriate to the material requirements planning environment. Alternative methods have therefore been developed for application to MRP which fall into three main categories which are fixed quantity safety stocks, safety times, and percentage increases in requirements.

(*i*) *Fixed Quantity Safety Stocks*

Fixed quantity safety stocks are introduced by triggering a net requirement whenever the projected stock on hand reaches a safety stock level rather than zero. Fig. 3.16 shows examples of MRP calculations with and without a fixed quantity safety stock.

The calculation of the size of the fixed quantity stock should be related to the cause of the unexpected usage during the lead time. For example, if the unplanned demand is primarily as a result of unforecasted spares demand for the item, than an historical analysis of this variation may lead towards the setting of a satisfactory safety stock level.

However, since in most cases variations in usage and supply could be the result of many factors and since there are not any 'scientific' methods of setting safety stocks in MRP systems,

Part No. C2218 H. Plastic Case LT=1 Safety Quantity=0

Week No.		13	14	15	16	17	18
Gross Requirements		200	300	200	400	300	500
Scheduled Receipts		—	—	—	—	—	—
Projected Stock on hand	600	400	100	0	0	0	0
Net Requirements		—	—	100	400	300	500
Planned Starts		—	100	400	300	500	—

(*a*) *Without Safety Stock*

Part No. C2218 H. Plastic Case LT=1 Safety Quantity=150

Week No.		13	14	15	16	17	18
Gross Requirements		200	300	200	400	300	500
Scheduled Receipts		—	—	—	—	—	—
Projected Stock on hand	600	400	150	150	150	150	150
Net Requirements		—	50	200	400	300	500
Planned Starts		50	200	400	300	500	—

(*b*) *With Safety Stock*

Fig. 3.16: The Effect of a Fixed Quantity Safety Stock

'rule of thumb' approximations have been applied. For example, it may be satisfactory to initially set the safety stock level at one week's average requirement or one week's 'maximum' requirement. However, it is essential that the usage of the safety stock is monitored and the level then adjusted accordingly *i.e.*, too frequent use of the safety stock would suggest the need for a higher safety level whereas infrequent use would suggest a lower one.

(ii) Safety Times

The safety time approach for setting safety margins in essentially 'planning to make items available earlier than they are required'. The intorduction of safety time is straightforward in that the net requirements are offset by the lead time and the safety time to produce planned starts. Fig. 3.17 shows examples of MRP calculations with and without a safety time.

Part No. C2218 H. Plastic Case LT=1 Safty Time=0

Week No.		13	14	15	16	17	18
Gross Requirements		200	300	200	400	300	500
Scheduled Receipts		—	—	—	—	—	—
Projected Stock on hand	600	400	100	0	0	0	0
Net Requirements		—	—	100	400	300	500
Planned Starts		—	100	400	300	500	—

(a) Without Safety Time

Part No. C2218 H. Plastic Case LT=1 Safety Time=1

Week No.		13	14	15	16	17	18
Gross Requirements		200	300	200	400	300	500
Scheduled Receipts		—	—	—	—	—	—
Projected Stock on hand	600	400	200	400	300	500	0
Net Requirements		—	—	100	400	300	500
Planned Starts		100	400	300	500	—	—

(b) With Safety Time

Fig. 3.17: The Effect of Safety Time

The choice of the length of the safety time could, perhaps, be related to the variability of the manufacturing or procurement lead time of the item being considered. However, since other factors may influence the use of the safety stock generated by the use of safe y time, an arbitrary setting of the safety time and subsequent adjustment based on the monitoring of the usage of the safety stock is satisfactory.

(iii) Percentage Increases in Requirements

The setting of safety margins by the percentage increases in requirements method is particularly suitable for dealing with the variations in supply caused by scrap or process yield losses and are often implemented as 'scrap factors' or 'shrinkage factors'. This type of safety margin is introduced by increasing the net requirements by a factor to produce planned starts. An example is shown in Fig. 3.18.

Part No. C2218 H. Plastic Case LT=1 Scrap Factor=0.05

Week No.		13	14	15	16	17	18
Gross Requirement		200	300	200	400	300	500
Scheduled Receipts		—	—	—	—	—	—
Projected on hand	600	400	100	0	0	0	0
Net Requirements		—	—	100	400	300	500
Planned Starts		—	105	420	315	525	—

Fig. 3.18: The Effect of a Scrap Factor

The size of the percentage increase in requirement should be directly related to the actual scrap or process yield loss for which it is supposed to be compensating. If this margin is to be used as a buffer against other variations then, again, an arbitrary setting may be made and subsequently modified based on the fee back of the actual use of the safety stock generated.

Safety stocks of finished products to provide a pre-determined customer service level should be set in the traditional fashion by analysing the operation of the sales forecast and translating the resulting requirements into a master schedule for the finished products.

9. Output Reports of MRP Systems

The principal outputs are the executive intructions to make or buy items in the form of requirements reports. Other, more specific reports may be produced such as 'projected on-hand summaries' 'projected shortages', 'expedite lists', 'cancellations' and 'supplier call-off schedules'.

Enquiries may also be made from the various input files, for example, from the bill of material, 'indented parts lists' and 'where used reports' could be obtained and from the inventory status file, 'stock status reports' and 'inventory analyses' could be generated.

In most companies the reports and their formats are specified to fit in with the particular organisational requirements.

10. The Implementation of MRP Systems

The problems that are likely to be encountered in the implementation of an MRP system may fall into many categories but their solutions will be dealt with briefly under two main headings, *i.e.*, analysis of the system task and user involvement and training.

(*i*) *Analysis of the System Task*

Before an MRP system its implemented or even proposed, a detailed feasibility study should be undertaken to determine:

(a) How 'standard' are the finished products?

(b) What would be the size and complexity of the bill of material?

(c) What would be the volume of modifications to the bill of material?

(d) How accurate is the current product structure information?

(e) How accurate are current inventory records?

(f) To what level of detailed control would stock condition records need to be taken?

(g) What length of planning horizon would be necessary?

(h) How easily can finished product demand be forecasted over this planning horizon?

(i) What would be the level of changes to the master schedule?

It the questions abve are investigated and answered satisfactorily at the feasibility study stage, then the implementation and eventual running of the system may encounter far fewer problems. Also, before implementation, user involvement and through user training are essential.

(ii) User Involvement and Training

The training should include an appreciation of the theory of MRP and more specific instructions for those who are likely to be involved in making particular decisions, for example, covering topics such as:

(a) The effect of changes to the master schedule

(b) The effect of batching

(c) The effect of safety stocks

(d) The importance of BOM accuracy

(e) The importance of stock recording accuracy etc.

Before implementation, it is also essential that the top management of the organisation clearly defines the responsibilities for the creation and maintenance of the data on the various computer files; it is seldom satisfactory to make this the responsibility of the data processing manager!

11. Conclusion

The benefits that can result from the use of a material requirements planning system can be considerable, some companies with successful implementations quoting:[2]

(i) Commonly 30 per sent reduction in component inventories

(ii) Better delivery performance and fewer stockouts

(iii) Up to 5 per sent increases in productivity

(iv) Up to 25 per cent less indirect employees engaged in stores, transport etc.

Apart from these sorts of benefits, MRP may also from the major input to other production planning and control subsystems in the organisation, for example.

(i) Shop loading (scheduling), where MRP already supplies the vital information of item quantities and required dates;

(ii) Capacity planning, where, with the addition of a routeing file (or bill of operations), detailed loads on departments and work centres can be produced for each period of the planning horizon.

In order to obtain the benefits offered by the use of MRP some organisations may have to change their business methods quite considerably. For instance, instead of accepting orders and quoting delivery dates based, to a large extent, on guesswork and then progressing these orders through the manufacturing departments by the use of 'shortage lists' and 'priority lists' the company may now have to attempt to forecast sales much further into the future, commit themselves to master schedules, commence production based on these schedules and than allocate customer orders, as they arrive, to the available unallocated products on the master schedule.

MRP has been used successfully in many different companies since the 1960s in the USA and since the early 1970s in the UK. It has applications in the manufacture of a wide variety of products ranging from aircraft engines to automobiles, from typewriters to machine tools, from batteries to generators and from lawnmowers to pharmaceuticals.

4

Materials Procurement

A. PROCUREMENT AS A MAJOR COST FACTOR

Materials procurement is the keystone in the supply cycle since it is the major source of the expenditures that are incurred. It is the process that converts plans and programmes into commitments to utilize resources. In business-oriented enterprises, responsibility for procurement is placed in a pivotal position because it directly affects operations and profits. In the government, the cost implications of materials procurement are not often fully recognized, as public accounting and budgeting systems usually obscure the relevant cost elements.

The cost elements can be described in relation to both the direct cost of goods and services obtained and the indirect costs incurred in the procurement process. Factors contributing to these cost categories include the follows:

(a) The word-wide search for potential sources of supply necessitated by the continuing dependence of most developing countries on imports;

(b) Invitations to tender evaluations, vendor selection processes and contract negotiations (the need for this expenditure may be considerably reduced by limiting the work involved to a few central co-ordinating agencies);

(c) Price of supplies and services obtained. Piecemeal buying has denied many governments price and benefits that can be derived from bulk purchasing; lack of effective price analysis and standard accurate pricing, which recovers all costs including overhead, is another major weakness;

(d) Inspection fees and adherence to specifications. Governments have been compelled to use third-party agents, consultants and contractors to strengthen their capability to enforce compliance with procurement specifications. This is partly the result of extensive imports from various countries that apply different standards and measures;

(e) Contracts and purchase order process. Procedural delays and fragmentation of the supply function in the government and the dependence on suppliers from different countries and sources have contributed significantly to this cost element;

(f) Freight and cargo-handling charges and indirect costs derived from: (i) delays in shipment; and (ii) delays in the discharge of cargoes at ports of destination resulting from inadequate cargo-handling facilities, cumbersome customs clearance procedures that impede onward distribution add and to the need and cost of carrying larger inventories; and

(g) Inventory control activities.

Another way to indicate the importance of materials procurement is to analyze the negative effects of poor materials procurements. Poor standards and ineffective quality control, delays in project implementation and wasted resources are typical results of inefficient procurement practices. To avoid or eliminate these weeknesses as well as to exercise effective measures to reduce costs, requires sound procurement organization, planning and procedures.

The above aims are not easy to achieve but such measures as:

(a) a sound system and arrangement for economic buying:

(b) the choice of right vendors and other contractors;

(c) well-defined specifications of the orders placed; and

(d) effective techniques for maintaining stocks at levels of economic and operational efficiency are part of the basic requirements that will ensure that goods and services are obtained and utilized in the most economic manner.

An effective system and procedure for timely shipments and cargo deliveries is another vital requirement. A separate chapter has been devoted to the analysis of the shipping and transportation aspects of supply management as they create unique problems for developing countries, especially those that depend substantially on imports.

B. APPROACHES TO RATIONALIZATION IN PROCUREMENT

A collective approach to procurement planning is a proven source of bargaining strength and economic buying. Integration of procurement planning responsibility with responsibility for development and administrative planning at the national level in some countries has enabled their governments to plan bulk purchasing with resultant economics, including trade concessions and reliefs. By the same token, substantial gaings have been achieved by integrating procurement planning at the departmental or sectoral levels with other relevant functional activities such as programme and production planning, financial control, accounting and staffing.

Where efficiency in supply management is a major concern, a central agency is sometimes established to plan, co-ordinate and execute procurement programmes and activities, for such common-use items as office supplies, house-keeping equipment, bulk supplies, maintenance tools, motor vehicles and standard spare parts. The General Service Administration in the Federal Government of the United States of America, the Korean Office of Supply, the Ghana Supply Commission, the Directorate of Supplies and Disposals in the Ministry of Supply in India and the Department of General Supply Management Affairs in Kuwait are examples of the centralized approach. In other cases where equipment and materials requirements are highly specialized, the responsibility for procurement planning and action is usually decentralized or assigned to agencies with the greatest need for the times involved and the ability to provide the necessary technical services, *e.g.*, ministries of health for medical supplies.

Whether the procurement responsibility is exercised by a central agency or by a decentralized authority, it is necessary that the organization concerned be in a position to exercise effective control and at the same time be protected from undue pressures from both internal and external interest groups, such as user agencies and vendors. They must be also able to influence government procurement policies and provide useful guidelines on procurement standards and procedures. To meet this important requirement, some governments have established standing procurement committees to support the individual agencies directly responsible for co-ordinating procurement work at different levels. One major advantage of the committee approach is that it provides a good opportunity for co-operation, exchange of ideas and collective commitment to decisions that have been reached.

1. Choice of Right Vendors

Identifying potential and reliable vendors and other supply and service contractors as well as maintaining up-to-date records on their suitability is vital to efficient procurement operations. It is essential that one should be able to distinguish recognized and well-established manufacturers and other suppliers' representatives from free-lancing agents; the latter have not always proved to be reliable.

The consequences of choosing the wrong type of supplier are serious both financially and operationally, and should therefore be avoided. The technical competence, managerial resources and financial capacity of potential suppliers must be proven to avoid unnecessary pitfalls. This can be achieved by ensuring that the following basic conditions prevail in each case that is considered:

(a) Satisfactory proof of the size and volume of orders that the supplier is capable of meeting; this should include particulars of the most recent largest orders satisfied;

(b) Delivery record should reflect minimum lead times and delays;

(c) Supplier's preparedness to accept the buyer's specifications and other important but reasonable contract conditions;

(d) Ability to respond rapidly to emergencies;

(e) The effectiveness of the supplier's organization and management, including the ownership status and operational reliability of plant and machinery;

(f) The firm's record of labour and industrial disputes and their effect on past performance in meeting demands must be positive;

(g) Conditions and facilities for after-sale services, especially in regard to the supply of space parts, equipment maintenance and repair facilities, must be satisfactory;

(h) Proven technical competence of the supplier's staff; and

(i) Financial capability of the supplier certified by a bank or some other recognized financial institutions. A supplier default may sometimes be more serious than a buyer's default.

2. Well-defined Specifications

Providing the means of ensure that the equipment and materials procured are of the right standard and quantity contributes significantly to measures that can be applied to control costs and increase efficieney in operations. These must be based on a system of specifications that defines clearly the minimum requirements of the composition, technical performance and perfect condition of each ordered item.

Specifications provide the key to standardization; the two together afe essential in establishing a basis for a common language and understanding in an activity that is characterized by a diversity of user demands and preferences. The need for clearity is strengthened by the wide variety of the same commodity resulting from technological changes, and the diversity of sources from which developing countries often obtain their supplies. Another important reason is the multiplicity of government agencies placing orders for goods.

In more advanced situations; technical specifications of commodities are established, and applied by user organizations as a standard in placing their orders. Established specifications also provide the means whereby purchasing agents are able to properly instruct suppliers. In addition, clearly defined specifications establish the guidelines that enable technical inspectors to test the quality and suitability of the goods in the process of manufacture and those receiced. Claims of users for failure by suppliers to comply with original requests have been easier to dispose of also because of established and clearly defined specifications.

3. Usefulness of Classifications, Coding and Cataloguing

Linked with the system of specifications and standardization are the classification, coding and cataloguing processes. These processes are administrative devices that facilitate the identification and retrieval of the numerous goods and commodities embraced by supply systems. Classification enables like items to be grouped together, as part of a process to eliminate duplication. Coding is the procedure for allocating symbolic identification marks to different items to simplify and facilitate their identification and retrieval. Following the increasing use of the electronic computer in data processing and information analysis to improve management, the development of numeric and alphabetic codes to identify discrete stock items, as well as groups and classes of commodities has become increasingly valuable. Cataloguing is the process of recording in the form of a comprehensive vocabulary, information on all classified and coded items; it serves as a ready reference and operating guide to both user departments, supply agencies, regulatory and control agencies and suppliers.

A complete and effective classification and coding system must meet certain basic requirements. For each stock item, the system should incorporate the following elements to facilitate identification:

(a) a unique uniform name or descriptive phrase; and

(b) a unique stock code number.

The name of an item is the key to its identification, source and use. In many supply systems the same item is often found to have different names and that has led to considerable confusion and duplication. Action to avoid this confusion has been taken in some countries and also by some international institutions in the form of glossaries of terms relating to a number of commodities in common use. Where two or more items happen to fall within the same name category, differentiation is achieved by a fine definition to highlight the unique characteristics of the item; *e.g.*, its colour, dimensions and shape.

The code number is a shortened form for identifying an item and provides the channel through which information on stock item can be conveniently and quickly stored, processed and retrieved. Coding is a complex and cumbersome process; it is therefore advisable that it be developed by skilled personnel. Inaccuracies in the codes assigned to the stock items will undermine any system designed to furnish management information on supply activities. Specialist consultants are usually employed to advise governments and organizations on materials classification and coding.

Developed and maintained properly, a classification, coding and cataloguing system will provide a standard mechanism to facilitate interagency transfer and exchange of stocks and thereby help to eliminate unnecessary and costly duplication in stock holdings. As in any other supply activity, this requirement can be properly met only when there is cooperation between supply management and other functions in the government. One approach to this is to establish a standing interdepartmental technical committee on standards and specifications to be serviced by a central supply agency. A major responsibility of the committee, where one exists, is to assist the central supply agency in developing and maintaining a standard materials and equipment catalogue.

C. APPROACHES TO MAINTAINING STOCKS AT ECONOMIC LEVELS

An efficient materials—procurement system includes the means to ensure that stocks are obtained and maintained at economic levels and in quantities that prevent interruption in the flow of needed resources. The aim is to avoid the negative effects of both excessive and insufficient inventories, which can be disruptive financially and operationally. Effective inventory control is therefore necessary to ensure adequate supplies and to keep the cost of procurement investments balanced against the consequences of stock-outs.

Excessive inventories are wasteful in that they generate unproductive use of capital and build up surplus stocks that may become obsolete. Unnecessary administrative and operational overhead such as charges for additional storage space handling, security and stock preservation also result from overstocking. Some tangible and intangible costs as well as other disadvantages also rasult from insufficient inventories. Frequent restorders leading to unnecessary overhead typify the negative effects of insufficient inventories. This overhead is often overlooked because it is hidden as a not readily measurable variable. Short inventories also result in delays in executing projects caused by short runs and increased set-ups to restart production, schedule interruptions and labour problems.

Whenever direct procurement costs and be identified, they should be included in the cost price of the item on order. Otherwise, indirect procurement costs should be distributed to item cost pricing by a suitable formula.

D. METHODS FOR ESTABLISHING ECONOMIC STOCK LEVELS

Several techniques, fotmulae can procedures have been established to effect inventory control, but for the purposes of this study, an abridged description of the Economic (Purchase) Order Quantity (EOQ) teehnique is provided, since it is widely used. To determine the most economic quantity to order, the technique requires that all inventory movement and stock level factors should be taken into consideration. In addition to the order price, order-processing cost and the cost of stock holding, the technique considers lead time, the rate of usage and the usage value of stock items. Other factors that the EOQ technique considers are the reorder point and the safety stock level.

1. Usage/Value Factor

The usage/value factor is a key guide in determining the size and frequency of the various orders that must be placed. This is based on the concept that additionai controls must be placed on higher-value stocks and on inventory items with the largest volume movement.

Inventories for different types of users may very considerably with the categories of stock items carried. However, experience demonstrates that about 20 per cent of all individual stock items in any inventory represent 80 per cent of the total inventory value. This means that the larger number of inventory items representing lower total value require a smaller investment to enlarge safety stock levels. Since larger inventories can be maintained, the time periods between reordering can be lengthened.

Conversely, the higher-value stock items require a high investment cost; safety stock levels should be as low as practicable; minimum economical purchases should be made; and physical verification of the book inventory should be carried out as frequently as possible. Although closer and more frequent controls on higher—value stocks are required, that does not mean that fewer controls should be exercised on the lower-value items.

The usage/value analysis procedure is known as the A-B-C system; it beings with the establishment of the classification of stocks in a descending order of values to provide different levels of control as illustrated below:

2. Lead Time—the Delay Factor

Lead time is the time that elapses between ordering goods, receiving them and placing them into use at the point of need. This delay factor includes the time required for assessing needs, as well as the time it takes to prepare and place the order. The time it takes the orders to reach the supplier, the time taken by the supplier to process the order and to ship the goods, and the time it takes the goods to be unloaded at the port of destination, discharged from the port and delivered to the user, are critical factors that the EOQ technique takes into consideration. Materials shipments as a factor of delay in the procurement create an important problem for developing countries.

Lead times are also influenced by fluctuations in usage rates; the more severe the fluctuations, the more difficult it is to

TABLE 4.1

Usage/Value Analysis—A-B-C System

Classtfica-tion	*Per centage of stock items*	*Percentage of value*	*Nature and level of control*
A	5	65	High usage low safety stock levels; frequent physical verification; minimum economic quantity ordered; close schedule control and review (daily, if possible).
B	15	15	Control not as tight as for "A" items, but tighter than for "C" items.
C	80	20	Low usage; high inventory levels; purchases in large quantities at less frequent interval« minimize clerical efforts to control; larger safety stocks; low stock-out risks.

stabilize the control. Therefore, buffer or safety stock levels can be established to cushion the effects of anticipated fluctuations. Inventory accounting records for each stock item should also differentiate between "balance-on-order" and "balance-on-hand".

3. Safe Stock Levels

The safe level of stock is dependent upon the rate of usage and the probability of shortage. Data on demand and usage trends provide the necessary guide in assessing the level of adequate stocks. Linked with adequate stocks and the rate of usage is the question of a safe reorder point. The reorder point is a predetermined signal marketing the point where action should be taken to provide enough time for replenishment to prevent stock-outs and unnecessary delays.

Safe stock levels can be calculated in various ways. One is by an arbitrary decision to set aside an approved reserve based on units of time, stretching from a few days to six months or longer, depending upon the type and value of goods, the item and the rate of usage. When new inventory accounting and reporting systems are installed, and usage histories and lead times are not known, this first approach may be the only alternative. Safe stock levels may be increased in proportion to the lead time, the assumption being that the longer the lead time, the greater the risk of a stock-out. This proportion can be established by setting "low" and "high" safe stock margins as illustrated the following table:

TABLE 4.2

Lead Time and Safe Stock Level

Lead time	*Safe stock level*	
	"*A*"	"*B*"
Up to 1 month	1 weeks' usage	2 weeks' usage
Up to 2 months	2 weeks' usage	1 month's usage
Up to 4 months	1 months' usage	2 months' usage
Up to 6 months	2 months' usage	3 months' usage

In instances where inventory accounting and reporting systems produce better information, safe stock levels can be more accurately predicted according to the following formulae:

$$DU=\frac{A}{365 \text{ days}}$$

$$MBOO=\frac{(Ld \times A)}{(365)}+S$$

$$MBOH=(DU \times LD)+S$$

A=annual usage requirements per item in units (metres, gallons, kilos)

S=safe stock margin or buffer

Ld=lead time in days

MBOO=minimum quantity required for balance on order and reorder point

MBOH=minimum quantity required for balance on hand and reorder point

DU=daily usage

Several formulae have been developed for the rapid calculation of the economic purchase order quantity. The following simplified formula is often used:

TABLE 4.3

Economic Purchase Order Analysis

$$EOQ=\sqrt{\frac{2\,AC}{IP}}$$

EOQ=economic Purchase order quantity in units;

A=annual usage requirements per item in units (metres, gallons, kilos);

C=cost of placing and receiving an order (clerical and handling processes);

I=inventory carrying cost (expressed as percentage of the average value of inventory);

P=purchase price per unit, including freight and discounts

A final and most important aspect of the measure to provide for efficiency and economy in the level of stocks that are maintained is that a system of physical control embracing a continuing stock-taking and regular auditing of stock records be maintained. This is necessary to ensure:

(a) accuracy in the quantity of stocks used and the balance on hand;

(b) continuing maintenance of proper and correct stock records;

(c) proper and optimum use of material resources including stocks reallocations and transfers; and

(d) prevention of the build-up of surplus stocks.

PRODUCTION PLANNING AND MATERIALS DECISIONS

Production planning may be defined as "the technique of foreseeing, and plotting in advance, all the steps in a series of operation in a manner that assures their accomplishment."

It predetermines what the work shall consist of, how it shall be accomplised, where it shall be performed, who shall do it, and when it shall be completed.

Four important techniques have been developed in order to assure a detailed accomplishment.

1. Routing, the plotting in advance of the path or spatial sequence of operations (how).
2. Scheduing, the plotting of a detailed timetable for operations (when).
3. Dispatching, the task of carrying out the routing and scheduling of materials (by whom).
4. Follow-up and Control, to control and make necessary adjustments after the programme has been put into practice.

All these four techniques will later be treated in detail.

Forecasting

In order to determine what the work shall consist of, many industries relay on a rather detailed forecasting of what the market wants, and what part of it the company might expect to achieve.

The following are the steps followed by a drug manufacturer:

1. The preparation of a sales forecast based on past sales and economic trends.
2. To align the sales forecast with the company's general inventory, and produce a manufacturing schedule,
3. To draw up materials-requirement sheets for the manufacturing schedules for use by the procurement department.
4. To prepare work orders (after procurement has been alerted about required delivery dates).

All companies must attempt to forecast their future business whether they manufacture to customers' orders or to stock. If manufacture is to order, forecasts are only for major over-all planning as it relates to prospective employment, machine and equipment needs, and financial requirements. These forecasts, expressed in some general measure such as pounds, tons, or man-hours, are essential to top-management policy making but do not directly involve the work of production planning and control department.

Forecasting is, however, closely related to production planning when production is to stock rather than to sales orders, especially in companies making products which take a long time to manufacture, like complicated assembled machines. Since products are made in advance of actual sale, failure to anticipate sales correctly causes shortages and lost sales, or overstocks which are costly to carry.

Forecasts of particular product demand are made only in campanies making a limited line of produets. Past sales are reviewed and forecasts of the sales of each product are made by the members of the sales department. The figures are adjusted in accordance with the forecast of general business conditions.

Seasonal variations in business must also be considered. They appear mostly in the clothing and shoe industry. It is important to try to level out production in order to reduce cost and maintain good labour relations.

Translating the Forecast into Terms of plant Capacity

Since the forecast is a forecast of sales, it automatically becomes a desired shipping schedule, because the month in which it is anticipated that the product will be sold, is the month in which it should be shipped. Since the finished products' inventory is to be held at a minimum, the desired shipping schedule is practically the same as a desired schedule for the last manufacturing operations. Steps to be followed in translating a desired assembly schedule into an approved schedule:

1. The capacity needed in the assembly department expressed in man-hours.
2. The man-hours needed to make parts and the time schedule in the parts departments.
3. Make necessary adjustments for making service parts, collateral parts, and other extras.
4. Compare the plan with the capacity available.

Advantages of Forecasting and Scheduling

1. Lower Cost

(a) Reduced cost of labour turnover.

(b) Increased plant efficiency with level production.

(c) More uniform quality with experienced help.

(d) Reduction of idle machine hours.

(e) Reduction of obsolescence through inventory policies and planned production.

(f) Adequate and economical raw material inventories.

(g) More efficient utilisation of storage space.

2. Improved Employee Relations

(a) More uniform hours of work per week throughout year.

(b) Better type of help attracted by stable employment conditions.

3. Improved Service to Customers

(a) Improved deliveries through inventory policies, bes utilisation of plant capacities and detailed scheduling.

(b) Better and more uniform quality of products.

4. The Need for Production Planning

The need for production planning as a separate activity and often as a separate department, is the result of the division of labour. The more a total production process is broken down into separate operations,all of which are mutually interdependent in making the finished product, the greater the need for bringing together and co-ordinating the planning of these operations in one central place.

There are four principal factors which make the adoption of scientific production-planning techniques necessary:

1. The complexity of modern production.
2. The need to determine definite completion times.

3. The need for co-ordination of all elements affecting costs.

4. The need for flexibility because of process changes.

The planning of what, where, when, how and by whom is the best known method for getting production results. Production at the lowest possible cost requires the maximum utilisation of men, machines and materials. The use of these three elements in conjunction with the planning factors, makes satisfied customers because of a fair price and delivry on time, and satisfied management because of low costs, minimum inventories and a smoothly operating organisation.

CONTROL FUNCTIONS AND PROCEDURES

Production plannning and control may be considered the nervous system of the factory. The complete and equipped factory is ready to function, yet without production control not one move is made, not one wheel is turned.

A continuous stream of directions must flow to the factory in order to have continuing, co-ordinated activity take place and to have completed products turned out in the desired form, quantity and quality; on time and within the limits of the cost permitted.

Production control almost always refers to the internal day-to-day direction of factory operations. The two main input factors in production are orders (from customer or sales department) and raw materials. Both orders and materials flow through the plant, and it is this flow that is being directed by the production control function.

Fig. 4.1 indicates how the production control is influencing all main activities in the company.

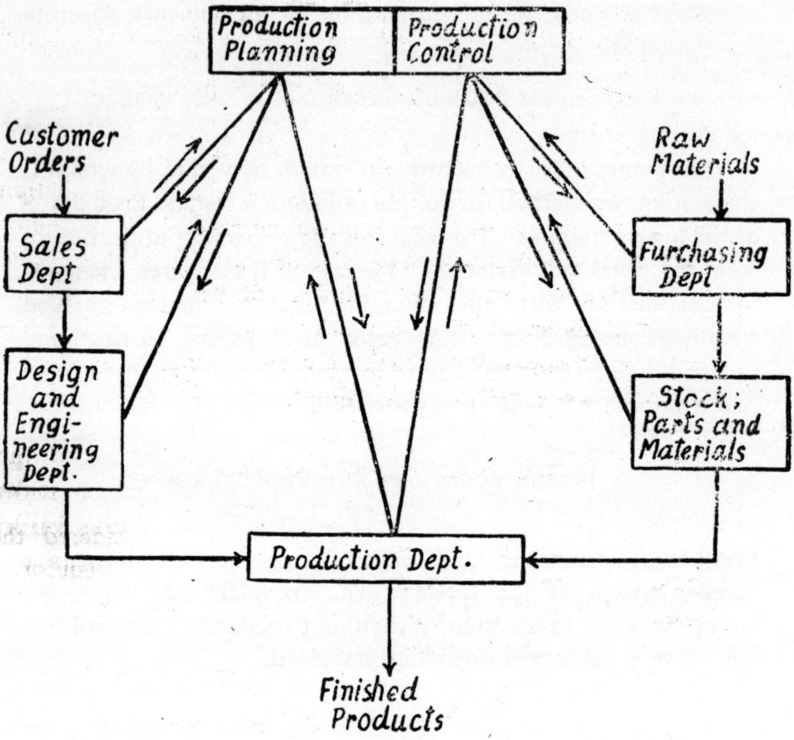

Fig. 4.1 : Production Planning and Control as the nervous system of the factory

1. Production Control Duties

Within the limits of the general objective of the company the production control activities are directed toward the following, more specific objectives;

(a) Optimum utilisation of men and their working time.

(b) The best possible utilisation of machines and equipment; technically and economically.

(c) Best possible utilisation of factory floor space.

(d) Aseure the presence of the right materials, at the right time, in the right place and in the right quantity and quality.

(e) Provide for a systematic flow of materials and parts between operations, minimising delays between work stations.

(f) Minimising capital requirement of keeping inventory.

(g) Assure that the required quantity of products is being delivered and that the quality is according to specifications.

(h) Make sure that promised delivery dates are being kept.

These duties of production control constitute some of the most important requirements to be fulfilled in order to make the company profitable in a competitive society.

2. Production Control Function

There are countless variations in methods of carrying out the work of production control, but rather few variations in the fundamental functions of that work. These functions apply to all manufacturing plants regardless of the nature of industry or the size of the company.

The major functions are as follows:

(a) Receive orders for products from sales department.

(b) Determine finished parts needed.

(c) Determine materials required.

(d) Maintain raw materials stock room.

(e) Determine operations required.

(f) Determine machines and machine attachment required.

(g) Determine the sequence of operations.

(h) Make up production orders.

(i) Make up production schedules.

(j) Make sure that all facilities for production will be available.

(k) Assign jobs to particular men and machines.

(l) Issue instructions of produce (dispatching).

(m) Control material transportation.

(n) Receive progress reports and evaluate performance.

(o) Replan when original plans are not carried out.

(p) Initiate remedial measures when original plans are not carried out.

(q) Control finished parts stock room.

(r) Control finished products stook room.

(s) Answer requests for information from sales department concerning delivery dates.

(t) Make estimates of costs of new jobs.

These functions, whether assigned to a production control department, are basic and must be done by some department in the organisation.

High volume repetitive work simplifies the performance of these function, while varied work complicates it.

When the functions are performed, how often, where in the organisation and how detailed they are being performed will vary, still they must be carried out sometime, somehow, by someone.

Other functions that may be associated with production control are:

Checking on shipping requirements (containers, etc.)

Instituting the use of palletes or other materials handling equipment.

Operating mail distribution service.

Standardisation of materials and parts.

These other functions are not essential, however, for the proper carrying out of the 20 basic functions listed above.

3. Production Control Procedure

Production control is, more or less, a matter of communication, and it must develop the procedure for the flow of information required. The production control department must know what information to send and what information to collect.

The various techniques used in the production control procedure are the subject of several lectures to follow in this course. It has already been pointed out that the procedure itself; *i.e.*, the method by which the basic information and the various techniques are used to control production vary greatly from one company to the other.

In the initial development of the procedure, however certain steps should be followed in order to succeed. In general the following four steps are required:

1. The collection and analysis of a series of production facts and relationships.
2. The rearrangement, organisation and systematisation of these facts and relationships.
3. The installation of an organised system for controlling production.
4. The refinement and changing of the system to make it operate smoothly.

The steps shall be outlined in some details:

A. COLLECTION AND ANALYSIS OF FACTS

1. Analyse the Product

(a) Analyse product design and specification. Consider the necessary co-ordination and co-operation between the production control department and design engineering.

(b) Develop if necessary an identification system so that each part, ingredient, raw material and final product has a unique number.

(c) Make a complete list of parts or ingredients identified by numbers.

(d) Analyse the materials used classify the materials for record keeping.

(e) Analyse the system of ordering, receiving, inspection and storing of materials. Analyse the methods of issuing and delivering materials of first operation.

(f) Write an operation sheet for each part.

(g) Study the method of estimating production costs.

(h) Analyse current inspection procedure.

Throughout the analysis of the product all facts and current practice should be questioned as to adequacy. Current procedure should be changed whenever necessary, and methods standardised wherever possible. Cost reduction possibilities should be searched for everywhere.

2. Analyse Plant Capacity

(a) Have a production layout made.

(b) Study the ability of the internal transportation system.

(c) Study the available machine tools for their economic relationships to production.

(d) Identify all department, process centres, tool cribs, stockrooms, machines and workplaces with a unique number or symbol.

(e) Prepare a file for a record of capacity, condition and productive constants for each machine.

In the plant capacity analysis the possibilities of rearrangements should be considered wherever this will accommodate the new plan. Possible replacement of machines and equipment should be considered as well.

3. Analyse Cost Accounting Procedure

(a) Analyse methods of collecting labour and material cost data.

(b) Discuss with cost accounting desirable changes for improving accuracy or speed of obtaining cost data.

4. Analyse Current Production Control System

(a) Make a process chart of the present flow of information used to control production.

(b) Study the current system to discover which parts to retain or discard.

During this stage of the analysis close co-operation is needed with design, cost accounting, purchasing, storekeeping, inspection and all levels of production department.

B. ORGANISATION OF THE PRODUCTION FACTS TO SOLVE CONTROL PROBLEM

1. Co-ordinate Sales Forecast with the Production Facilities

(a) Translate sales forecast into requirements for raw materials.

(b) Determine the rate of production for the various parts necessary to satisfy the sales forecast.

(c) Determine if present production capacity is adequate, or whether subcontracting is necessary.

2. Organise a System for Inventory Control

(a) Determine proper inventory levels.

(b) Develop system of releasing purchasing or manufacturing order to maintain proper level.

3. Develop Lot Size Formulas and Charts

4. Organise the Scheduling Procedure

(a) Schedule the major steps necessary for completing a new product ready for production.

(b) Schedule the production cycles for all materials or units going into this product.

(c) Schedule the production of all parts requested by the inventory control system.

(d) Devise special methods of scheduling where desirable.

5. Accumulate Machine Loads for all Scheduled Orders

6. Develop Standard Forms and Controls to Co-ordinate Activities

(a) Mount control board where needed.

(b) Show how orders, returns and reports are routed.

(c) Select method of reproducing the forms required.

7. Set up the Dispatching Groups

(a) Dispatching procedure.

(b) Dispatching Stations.

(c) Internal transportation and its control.

C. INSTALLATION OF THE PLAN

The plan may be installed in the entire plant on a certain date, or installed in one department or a group of related departments on a certain date.

In either case the following steps are necessary:

1. To change over all records of inventories, production, tools etc., to the new forms.
2. To schedule and have short meetings in order to inform and explain the changes to supervisors etc.
3. To start all control working.
4. To issue procedure instructions.
5. To have personnel available that can answer questions and aid in the operation of the plan.

D. MODIFICATION OF THE PLAN

1. Watch the Trouble Points and Analyse the Cause

(a) Revise methods, duties and functions wherever needed.

2. Watch Forms, Returns and Reports to Determine Whether Information is needed or used

3. Collect Records of Performance

(a) Changes in direct labour hours per unit.

(b) Percentages of promises kept.

(c) Percentages of plant capacity used per unit of product before and after production control.

(d) Effect of new inventory control system on material shortages or surpluses and capital investment.

Many of the topics outlined will be analysed and discussed in detail throughout the course.

5

Flow Control of Materials

GENERAL

The term flow control is used to describe the type of production control exercised in continuous production. Flow control deals with incoming materials delivery schedules, production rate control and outgoing shipment schedules. (While order control is primarily an internal control dealing with individual orders and operations.)

The tremendous volumes often encountered in continuous production require close matching of incoming materials and shipment with production rate.

Production control in the ideal continuous production, *i.e.*, completely standardised steady rate production, is comparatively simple. Since the stream of goods produced is usually not altogether homogeneous, however, it turns out to be more complicated.

PROCESSING AUTHORITY

Processing authority in continuous production is extremely important, yet it is hardly evident in the day-to-day production.

It this type of production processing authority is built into the equipment to a great extent.

The initial process authority is almost always issued by the engineering department. (The selection, design and placement of machines, the instructions covering how to perform the job, how to set the machine, what attachments to use, etc.)

When this initial processing authority is once made, no or only a small amount of additional specifications would be required to tell factory personnel how to do the job.

ROUTING

Most of the work of routing is embodied in the product design, the design of machines and the arrangement of the machines.

Once this routine has been done, it can hardly be changed without making complete rearrangements of the entire line. Even the exact movements of operators are often predetermined and specified by the methods engineer, and workers must follow their instructions in order to be able to keep up.

PRODUCING AUTHORITY

Production programme releases is the usual from of producing authority in continuous production using flow control.

The release covers usually a one-week period and is determined at least one month in advance.

ASSEMBLY CONTROL

Once the assembly line has been set up to handle the desired rate of flow, the control of production is chiefly a matter of feeding parts and sub-assemblies to the various work areas at the rate and time required.

The guaranteeing of material at the assembly line when needed may be accomplished by two methods; by stock banks along the line or by delivery conveyors or feeding lines.

A. Stock Banks Along the Line

Relatively small items to be used in assembly are often stored at the various stations along the line, and at the head of the line.

Material may be placed beside the operators, directly on the workbench or in bins in front of the operator.

Special stock men are instructed to maintain the supply at a level that will be enough for a stated period of time. (Safety bank.) Sometimes all parts for an assembly are stored at the head of the line and placed in one container being moved down the line.

If similar but different parts are being used at the same work station, they must be clearly identified.

B. Delivery Conveyors

Bulky stuff cannot often be stored along the line itself.

Continuously circulating conveyors are often used.

Ordinarily they are set up to hold a number of parts and to circulate at a rate fast enough to that operators need not wait for stock. He takes off only as much as he requires and lets the rest go by. Handlers are instructed to replenish emptied hooks or carriers.

Automatically indexing conveyors of the endless type accomplish the same end. The conveyor stops itself when the stock is in the decided position and indexes itself when the piece is removed.

Feeder line and delivery conveyors may be scheduled to the assembly line by adjusting speed according to speed of assembly line.

A variety of parts, colours or models may be scheduled over any of the two last mentioned types of delivery conveyors (indexing or synchronised delivery conveyors).

The only problem is the loading of the parts in correct sequence.

Unique numbers must be assigned to each assembly and to the parts going into this assembly.

PARTS CONTROL

Wherever parts are produced continuously their production rate must match the rate of use on an over-all basis.

Usually the capacity of part production line must be greater than assembly needs, because of repair parts etc.

Operating schedules for parts made continuously are only statements of rates per hour and hours per day.

Frequent reports and "count" points are often needed to ensure that part production matches the usage in assembly line.

Most parts must be produced in lots, however, because of the fact that most machine operations are generally much faster than the rate of assembly. Order control may be used but is usually unnecessary.

Cycling is the most common way of controlling part production on lot basis.

Cycle in this connection means the complete rotation through one machine of all different items that are to be made by this machine. The cycling time is the number of days allowed for one cycle.

Example: One machine may produce one month's supply of four different parts during one month. The runs of the four different parts, in the same sequence, are then repeated every month, keeping the volume constant and the match the usage of the parts in the assembly line.

PROCUREMENT CONTROL

Most continuous production companies receive enormous quantities of materials and parts. Incoming supplies must often be scheduled to arrive at certain times in the day. The purchasing department is usually responsible for the location of vendors who can ensure a steady and dependable flow of materials required.

The vendor, who often has to time his own schedule of delivery to the programme set by the manufacturer, must be notified ahead of time what, when and how much will be called for. Vendors must be investigated and checked continuously by planning and production engineering people who make sure that the estimated delivery can be realised.

Frequently orders for one product are spread over two or more vendors, for protection purposes, but careful selection of vendors is considered more important and more discriminating a precaution.

The vendor is usually notified of the desired delivery schedule (what, when and how much) and is held responsible for meeting the schedule.

Follow-up clerks are constantly checking the receipts against requirements, and are recording all pertinent facts concerning vendors' reliability:

shipping instructions;

shipments made by vendors;

" received;

promises made;

scrap, shrinkage or returned materials, etc.

SHIPMENT CONTROL

In high volume continuous production the production control is often responsible for moving finished products out of the plant as well.

Packing and loading freight cars may be part of this responsibility.

FLOW CHART SCHEME

A. PRODUCTION PLANNING—PROCESS PLANNING —MATERIAL FORM AND QUANTITY

Introduction

Work to be Done

1. Design fixes the final state of materials.
2. Very often the initial from and shape can be varied.
3. With some classes of material the design specification does not indicate the amount of material required and this must be calculated.

Different Material Forms for Same Product

1. Gears: bar blank, rough forging, drop forging.
2. Castings: different proportions of pig, scrap and ladle additions.

3. Animal feeding stuffs: different ingredients for some product.

The Choice Between Alternatives

1. Cost (Total, Marginal, Direct).
2. Operational research approach.

The Material Schedule (or list of material quantities)

1. Unit lossess (*e.g.*, one cutting off and two facing allowances in bar work).
2. Batch losses (*e.g.*, "short end" in bar work, too short for chuck).
3. Tabulation of material requirement per unit of output.

Design Analysis

Many of the decisions concerning material form and shape affect others beside the process planner; better considered by a committee as part of design analysis.

Production Control and Material Quantity

Better material utilisation with single phase flow than with multi phase flow. For example, in sheet metal work it is cheaper in material and in labour if sheet utilisation is planned to cut product sets of components from the sheet.

Summary

B. PRODUCTION PLANNING—PROCESS PLANNING
THE CHOICE OF PLANT

Introduction

Three Different Problems

1. New plant for new factory.

2. Replacement plant.
3. Selection between existing plant to do an operation.

New Plant for new Factory

1. Appraisal of a possible plant item.
   - (a) Will it do the job? (right process, size, power, etc.).
   - (b) How long will it take? (operation time)
   - (c) How much will the plant cost?
   - (d) How much will it eost to operate?
   - (e) How much will it cost to instal? (Foundations, new power cables, additional services, etc.)
   - (f) How much will it cost to maintain? (Spares, service)
   - (g) Does it require special skills to operate or maintain?
   - (h) How long will it take to set up?
   - (i) What is the delivery?
   - (j) How long will it last?
   - (k) Resale value and/or alternative uses (flexibility).
   - (l) Select Possible, alternatives for each purpose.

Note: Often when appraising plant one may find ways in which routes could be amended with advantage by changing method.

2. The comparison of alternatives.
   - (a) Rating (simple and weighted points systems).
   - (b) Budget filling (obtaining the best value for a given sum).
   - (c) Economic analysis.

Economic Analysis in Plant Selection

1. Annual cost method (reduces all receipts and expenditure to a cost series).
2. Present worth method (finds equivalent capital sum).
3. Rate of return method (finds marginal return on marginal investment).
4. "M.A.P.I." method. (Adds "operating inferiority" and "capital cost" over a time series, to find "adverse minimum").

Replacement Plant

Exactly the same approach except, that one of the items compared is an existing item of plant.

Selection between Existing Plant for an Operation

1. Will it do the job?
2. How long will it take?
3. How long will it take to set up?
4. Will the choice affect the material flow efficiency?
5. Will the choice affect the balance of load?

If the plant layout is good, this problem should never arise. The correct machine will be obvious due to its position. It is only if the layout is bad that the selection is difficult.

Summary

C. PRODUCTION PLANNING—PROCESS PLANNING —MATERIAL HANDLING

Introduction

Principles

1. Eliminate all unnecessary handling moves by simplification of design and process planning. (*i.e.*, reduce

number of components and operations to reduce handling moves).

2. Reduce the distance and difficulty of necessary handling moves by efficient plant layout.
3. Eliminate all double handling.
4. Use gravity where possible. (It's free power).
5. Mechanise all remaining transfers.
6. Use "unit loads" where applicable and possible.
7. Standardise equipment and develop unified methods.

Planned Handling

1. In factory planning classify items to be handled and specify handling system for each class.
2. In process handling, study each component and its handling moves and specify:

   (a) The containers or unit loads to be used.

   (b) The handling equipment required.

   (c) The method.

Handling Systems

A handling system consists of a combination of a particular load type and handling equipment, with a specified method of use. Examples are:

1. Without Containers

(a) Gases, with pumps and pipes.

(b) Liquids, with pumps and containers.

(c) Single pieces, with chutes, conveyors, cranes.

2. With Containers (gasses, liquids and bulk materials)

(a) Gases, in vessels, on lorries.

(b) Liquids, in tanks, on rail wagons.

(c) Cement, in paper sacks, on conveyors.

3. *Piece Parts in Batches in Containers*

(a) Boxes, bins, trays, etc., with trolleys, trucks, trailers, etc.

(b) Stillages (skids), with lift trucks.

(c) Pallettes, with fork trucks.

(d) Strapped unit loads, with fork trucks.

(e) Boxes, with conveyors, etc., etc.

Relationship between Handling and Processing

1. Combination of handling move and operation, *e.g.*, weathering, paint dipping, etc.
2. Mechanical transfer between operations (automation).

Relationship between Handling and Storage

1. Conveyor storage.
2. How storage racks with gravity feed to dispensing station.

Classification of Handling Equipment for Piece Loads

Main classes: cranes, conveyors, tractors and trailers, trucks, R.R. equipment, tiering machines, lifts and hoists, monorails, pneumatic and hydraulic systems, chutes, industrial storage facilities, process handling equipment.

Planning the Industrial Handling Move

1. Define the job to the done.
2. Select the route.

3. Calculate the frequency of transfers.
4. Measure the distance.
5. Measure the speed of travel.
6. Select the container.
7. Select the equipment.
8. Specify the method.

Summary

D. PRODUCTION PLANNING—PROCESS PLANNING—
"TYPES OF LAYOUT"

Introduction

Types of Layout

1. Line layout.
2. Group layout.
3. Functional layout.
4. Flexible layout.

Line Layout

1. Line layout for single major components.
2. Balancing the line:
   (a) Additional machines.
   (b) Doubling (one operates two machines).
   (c) Process development.
   (d) De-rating (cheaper machines, greater reliability).
   (e) Additional work under-utilised operations (*e.g.*, fettling).
   (f) Branch lines and machines shared by two lines.

Line layout for families of similar components.

(a) Division into "families" (by eye, classification).

(b) Setting-up time the main limitation.

(c) Examples.

4. Advantages of line layout.

(a) Minimum stock.

(b) Minimum throughput time and delivery.

(c) Minimum direct cost.

(d) Minimum indirect costs (handling control, administration).

(e) Maximum quality (consistency, shorter warning of errors).

Group Layout

1. Division into groups (one group per family of parts).
2. Layout inside group area.
3. Advantages of group layout. Some as line layout, but lower in degree.
4. Group layout, the first step towards line layout.
5. Examples.

Functional Layout

1. Division into sections.
2. Layout inside sections.
3. Advantages—often only apparent.
4. Disadvantage—high stocks, complicated control and administration.
5. Examples—everywhere. This is the traditional form.

Flexible Layout (examples: press work, garment assembly).

Automation

Line flow, plus automatic material transfer, plus automatic process control.

The line of progress is clear. "Functional", to "group", to "line", to "automation". Sometimes one can jump.

Summary

Although line layout and automation are the ultimate aim in any layout work, there are sometimes practical limitations which prevent its use in particular situations, at particular stages in technological development.

E. PRODUCTION PLANNING—PROCESS PLANNING—
PLANT LAYOUT

Introduction

Routing Analysis

1. Check load and estimate plant requirement.
2. Select items suitable for line layout.
3. Use grouping analysis, to see if groug layout is possible:
   (a) Strip analysis.
   (b) Punched card methods.
   (c) Classification and coding systems.
4. Check effect of different solutions on plant requirement.
5. Modify routes, etc., to improve solution.

Selection of Plant

1. Select plant and prepare specifications.
2. Place orders.

Services

1. List all services required (*e.g.*, power, light, gas, compressed air, water, coolants, lubricants, waste removal).
2. Plan systems of distribution with particular attention to flexibility (*e.g.*, bus bars for electricity, plugs for compressed air, etc.).

Layout Techniques

1. Sketches and drawings.
2. Templates (card, magnetic, plastic, etc., printing methods).
3. Models.

Layout Plant

1. Sketch alternatives, select the best.
2. Estimate area requirements round work centres.
3. Make trial layout.
4. Check flow—string diagram.
5. Check services—modify supply system.
6. Criticise and improve.

Check List

Develop a check list of things to remember and check. Learn your own weaknesses, remember previous errors and keep them on the list. Typical check list items:

1. Safety: does the layout introduce hazards from flying chips? danger of fire? can the building be evacuated quickly? danger from crane borne loads.
2. Material handling: can I get materials to and from all machines? can scrap be removed easily?
3. Maintenance: is there access to all machines for maintenance? could all machines be moved out for repair if necessary?
4. Officers: is there provision for those who have to do writing as part of their jobs? are there too many offices?

Plant Layout in an Existing Factory

1. First study existing layout, make flow diagram, learn about its weaknesses.
2. Then follow exactly the same sequence of work as described above, including a review of the existing plant, and recommendations for changes.
3. Attempt to develop a layout which will not necessitate major moves of heavy plant and the re-arrangement of services.
4. Start by planning the ideal arrangement, and then modify it as little as possible to make it fit the existing limitations.

Summary

F. PRODUCTION PLANNING—PROCESS PLANNING—ASSEMBLY LAYOUT

Introduction

Assembly

1. Four factors: plant, labour, materials and the assembly itself.

2. Forms of assembly (plant and labour usually together).
3. Types of layout (principal types: "line" and "fixed centre").

Choice of Layout Type

Choose line layout unless:

1. The planned output requires less than two assemblers.
2. The bulk or weight of the assembly, or materials, is too great for economical handling.
3. There are technical reasons why the product must be assembled in one position (base plates, heavy jigs, controlled atmosphere, safety).

Planning Line Assembly Layout

1. Assembly build chart—showing sequence of assembly.
2. Estimate labour required for main line, and divide work into that number of operations.
3. Estimate labour required for sub-assemblies. Where one or more operators is required for a sub-assembly, (or convenient group of sub-assemblies), plan a branch line. (All other sub-assemblies list for separate treatment).
4. Plan services and handling methods.
5. Sketch alternative layouts and choose the best.
6. Prepare trial layouts: criticise and improve.

Methods of Moving "Assembly"

1. Sliding.
2. Trolleys.
3. Roller track and wheel track.
4. Conveyors.

Methods of Delivering Material to Lines

1. Racks at work stations.
2. Pallets or boxes to work stations.
3. Overhead conveyors to work stations.
4. Issue on main track in product sets from a "marshalling store".

Planning Fixed Centre Layout

1. List all assemblies to be produced and/or divide into types by: bulk, weight, services required, special skills, etc.
2. Specify standard equipment (bench, universal vice, etc.).
3. Estimate areas and sketch work centre layout.
4. Estimate times and calculate number of work centres required.
5. Plan services and handling methods.
6. Sketch alternative layouts and choose the best.
7. Prepare trial layout; criticise and improve.

Methods of Delivering Materials to and from Centres

1. Racks at work centres.
2. Pallets or boxes to work centres.
3. Conveyors to work centres.

Summary

G. PRODUCTION PLANNING—PROCESS PLANNING—STORES LAYOUT

Introduction

Stock Classification (Know your stock!)

1. Classify by size. (Bar, common parts, provision for bulky items.)

2. Classify by products. (Important for assembled products.)
3. Classify by demand frequency. (Retail, wholesale, general.)
4. Classify by fragility and special hazards.
5. Develop main classifications.

Principles of Storage

1. Eliminate need to store where possible.
2. As a second alternative consider flow storage (integrated handling and storage).
3. Store in unit loads where possible.
4. Take advantage of height (stocks and racks).
5. Minimise handling of high demand frequency items.
6. Minimise storage space for low frequency demands.
7. Combine storage with processing (*e.g.*, packing).
8. Provide special facilities for: inflammables, contaminants, security items, and perishable items.

Storage Equipment

1. Conveyors.
2. Flow line storage racks.
3. Pallets (floor storage).
4. Racks (for pallets and free loads).
5. Bins (and again racks to take them).

Planning the Storage Layout

1. Tabulate information:

   (a) Scope of work (include goods receiving or packing?)

(b) Building plans (all stanchions, lifts, windows, floor loading, etc.).

(c) Stock volume (maximum and minimum).

(d) Receipt and issue composition and frequency.

(e) Items requiring special attention (inflammable, security, perishable, co-conta).

(f) Available handling and storage equipment,

2. Choose containers (pallets, bins, etc.).
3. Choose racks.
4. Choose handling equipment.
5. Sketch alternative layouts, and choose the best.
6. Make trial layout, criticise, develop and adopt.

Check List

Develop a check list of points to watch, *e.g.*:

1. Office: Is the storekeeper well placed to check incoming and outgoing loads, unauthorised visitors, etc.?
2. Gangways: Are they the right width for the handling equipment? Is there provision for the circulation of traffic?
3. Safety: Does layout introduce any special hazards? Is there a fire risk? Have I provided special facilities for inflammables, corrosives, explosives, etc.?
4. Stock checking: Could stock checking be facilitated by a change in layout or equipment?
5. Height: Have I used the full height available?
6. Frequency: How near are the high frequency items to the despatching point?

Summary

H. PRODUCTION PLANNING– OPERATION PLANNING

Introduction

Scope of Operation Planning

1. Plan the method.
2. Design the tooling.
3. Design or select subsidiary equipment.
4. Layout the work centre.
5. Specify operating procedure and estimate standard time (M.T.M.).

Plan the Method

1. List elements and plan best sequence.
2. Check by motion analysis, at least for complicated operations.
3. Specify method.

Design the Tooling

Different for each different process technology, but the principles are the same:

1. Design to attain standards set in product specification.
2. Design for minimum operation time.
3. Design for minimum setting time.
4. Design for ease of pre-setting (to conserve capacity).
5. Design for minimum cost of tool production.
6. Design for ease of maintenance and repair.
7. Design for ease of handling and storage.
8. Use standard tools and tool parts where possible.

9. Design for maximum return on investment (suitability for rate).

Design or Select Equipment

1. Handling of incoming materials and transfer to work centre.
2. Handling of finished items and transfer from work centre.
3. Handling during work cycle (manipulators, etc.).
4. Waste disposal.
5. Hand tools and suspension devices.
6. Service equipment (steam, compressed air, vacuum lines, etc.).
7. List all equipment required.

Layout of the Work Centre

1. Sketch possible layouts, choose the best, develop, criticise and improve.
2. Fix positions for incoming and outgoing materials.
3. Fix positions for all tools.
4. Check for operator's comfort.
5. Check for ease of maintenance.
6. Check for safety.
7. Check for ease of waste removal.
8. Check for ease of work checking (quality control).

Specify Operating Procedure and Estimate Standard Time

1. Enter details of method, tools and equipment on "operation sheet".
2. Estimate standard time:

(a) Experience.

(b) Synthetic times.

(c) Laboratory times,

(d) Time study after work starts.

3. Enter standard time on "operation sheet".

Summary

I. PRODUCTION PLANNING—REVIEW

Introduction (considers the production unit of factory).

Content

1. Decides how to make this product.
2. Starts with an aim.
3. Divided for convenience progressively into:

   (a) Factory planning (process, departments and classes of material).

   (b) Process planning (operations, work centres and components).

   (c) Operation planning (elements, work stations and components).

4. At each stage we consider:

   (a) The sequence of work tasks.

   (b) The spatial relationship between work places.

Factory Planning

1. Make or buy policy.
2. Division into process departments.

3. The provision of stores, service departments, power services, etc., and officers.
4. Materials handling policy.
5. Factory layout.

Process Planning

1. Make or buy.
2. Routing.
3. Material form, shape and quantity.
4. Materials handling details.
5. Plant layout in the department.

Operation Planning

The detailed planning of the work operation; of the tooling and of the layout of each work centre.

The Sequence of Planning

1. Three approaches to problem.
   (a) As described in this course with progressive application.
   (b) As described in this course, but complete planning before application, and modify earlier decisions as necessary and desirable.
   (c) Reverse order. (Do operation planning first).

2. Depends on type of product.
   (a) For one product, mass production lines, which are completely new, use methods (b) or (c).
   (b) For general purpose batch production plants, where flexibility is essential use method (a).

Production Planning in Existing Plants

1. All the same steps must be considered.
2. Determine what is being done now.
3. Determine the ideal.
4. Make the best compromise.

General Principles

The principal indicators of good production planning are: the type of flow and the cost of production. If production planning is done well, all other planning is simplified and made cheaper and more effective.

Relationship with Work Study

Production planning makes the plans. Work study keeps them under continual review and improves the methods where possible.

Summary

J. PRODUCTION CONTROL—TIME—STANDARD TIME

Introduction

Work Study

Method study pules time study.

Time Study

1. Preliminary study.
2. Division into elements.
3. Timing the elements ("Recorded element times").
   (a) Continuous method.
   (b) Snap-back method.

(c) Repetitive method.

(d) Cycle method.

4. Selecting the element time ("Selected element time").

   (a) Strike out abnormal times.

   (b) Average method.

   (c) Minimum method.

   (d) Model Method.

   (e) Good time method.

5. Performance rating (to find "basic operation time").

   (a) Levelling factors.

   (b) Rating scales.

6. The addition of allowances.
7. Specify standard time for operation ("standard time").

Synthetic Times (Manual operations)

1. The Gilbreths and their "therbligs".
2. Predetermined—elemental—time standards.
3. Methods—time measurement, work-factor system, etc.

Synthetic Times (Machine operations)

1. Development.

2. Advantages.

Summary

K. PRODUCTION CONTROL—TIME—CONSUMPTION, THROUGHPUT, IDLE AND WAITING TIME

Introduction

Batch Life (considers materials and time)

The time during which a batch of material is in existence, in a specified segment of the flow system is the "batch life".

1. It starts when the order is issued.
2. It ends when the last item is consumed.

Analysis of Batch Life

1. Preparation time.
2. Throughput time.
   - (a) Waiting time.
   - (b) Process time.
3. Preparation time plus throughput time=lead time.
4. Consumption time.

Estimating Lead Time and Throughout Time

1. Related to process time: relationship changes with flow type, load and scheduling efficiency.
2. The relationship can be found by direct analysis of records.
3. Arbitrary factors to convert from process time.
4. Statistically controlled factors.

Machine Idle Time (considers machines and time)

1. Time when machine is not doing useful work.

(a) Ancillary time (setting-up, cleaning, etc.).

(b) Machine idle time (no work, no operator).

(c) Down time (machine broken down).

(d) Inoperative periods (at night, weekends, etc.,).

2. Recorders and frequency studies.
3. Capacity (standard machine running time).

Labour Idle Time (considers labour and time)

Time when labour is not doing useful work.

Summary

6

Materials Scheduling

Manufacture involves the processing or fashioning of materials in order to produce an article. The processes to be performed must, in most cases, be carried out in a particular sequence or pattern. If, for example, a product contains a number of parts which have to be assembled together, no product can be completed until a set of parts is available. Ideally, the manufacture of the parts themselves must be started at points in time which allow their completion on the same date. If the times for manufacture differ then the determination of the individual manufacturing start dates involves working back from the planned start date for assembly. This is illustrated diagrammatically in Fig. 6.1. The diagram shows that component B must go into manufacture first, followed by A,E, and so on. The length of the horizontal lines is proportional to the time required for manufacture, drawn against a common scale of days, hours, weeks, etc., as required.

Each batch of components may involve several operations, and these will generally have to be arranged for consecutive performance. If sub-assembly is to take place before final assembly, it will sometimes involve similar consecutive operations. In other cases it may be possible to have work performed on several different kinds of sub-assembly consecutively.

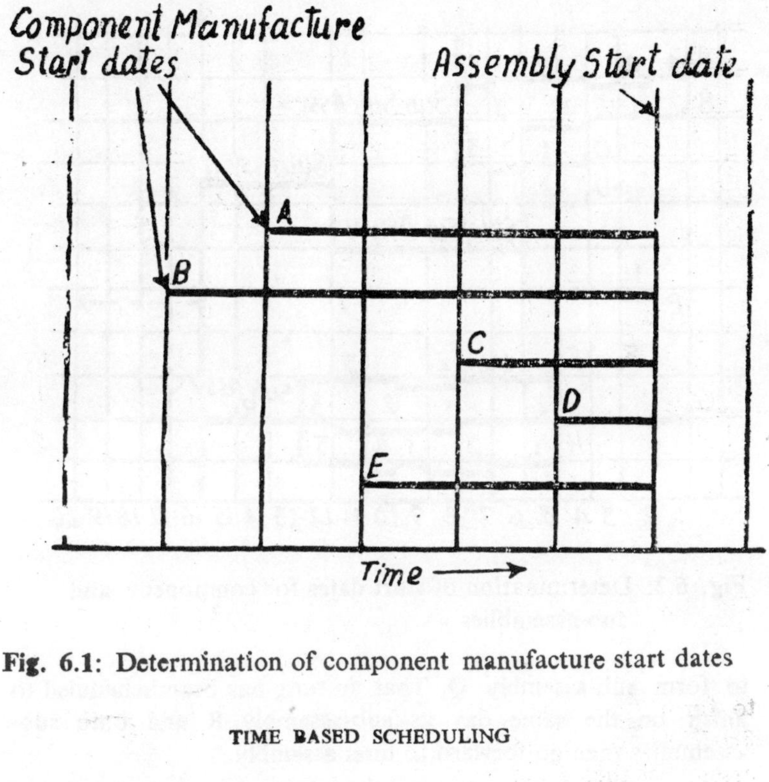

Fig. 6.1: Determination of component manufacture start dates

TIME BASED SCHEDULING

Reference to Fig. 6.2 will illustrate the principle involved in the process of arranging start dates for the various steps in manufacture. Assume that the components are made in sets suitable in quantity to make one finished assembly and that machining and assembly operations occupy multiples of whole days. The components A require four operations occupying one, two, three and one days each. The set will be completed at the end of day 7. B requires the same number of days and is thus started on the same day as A, and C requires only four days and must be started on day 4. The three sets of components will be completed at the end of day 7 and go to sub-assembly for sub-sub-assembly X to be started. That will take four days. Sub-sub-assembly Y has been scheduled to complete on the same day as X and the two sub-sub-assemblies are then put together

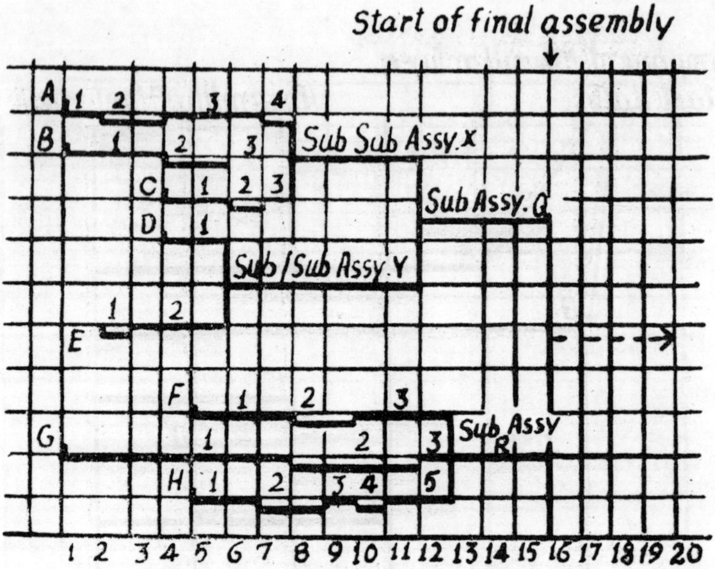

Fig. 6.2: Determination of start dates for components and sub-assemblies

to form sub-assembly Q. That in turn has been scheduled to finish on the same day as sub-assembly R and both sub-assemblies then go forward to final assembly.

Clearly if the times shown apply only to enough components to make one final assembly and more than one is required, it will be necessary either to allow more time or to increase the number of machines or men involved in order to follow the time scale given. Equally it would not usually be necessary to wait until, for example, all the sub-assemblies Q and R were finished before starting on the first final assembly. In flow manufacture conditions material would be fed in at a rate and capacity would be provided which would permit the continuous production of finished assemblies.

If the chart (Fig. 6.2) showed the time scale required for the production of, say, one hundred final assemblies. the then times required for fractions or multiples of one hundred can be calculated with a reasonable degree of precision.

This process, which is known as scheduling, thus provides the outline of a manufacturing plan which can be operated in ideal conditions. That is to say when no other work will obstruct its completion. Within such a plan or schedule, reasonable allowance must be made for interruptions caused by machine breakdown, scrap, or delays or wasted time from other causes. The amount of contingency time allowed and built into the plan will be determined on previous recorded experience.

It is important to note that the schedules given as examples in Figs. 6.1 and 6.2 are time based and are not referred to any particular date. If Fig. 6.2 is taken to apply to one final assembly and if the plan can be put into operation without alteration starting on any particular date, then final assembly will be able to start at the beginning of day 16.

OUTPUT BASED SCHEDULING

If the machines involved in a manufacturing process have a known output per hour in terms of numbers of parts or metres of material it may prove more convenient to prepare schedules based on quantity rather than time. However, this type of scheduling is fundamentally the same as that already described since output is basically always related to time even if it is sometimes desirable to express it in other terms for particular purposes.

MANUFACTURING FOR STOCK

Once the designs of a product which it is intended should become a standard line have been finalised, it is possible to prepare a master schedule along the lines already indicated. This implies that the design has been proved and that a pilot batch has passed through the manufacturing process. Special tools and tooling will have been put into use and modifications made, where necessary, to manufacturing methods, sequences and, very probably, times.

Up to this point the master schedule will have been tentative and subject to modification in the light of experience gained with the pilot batch or batches. Strictly speaking, however; it is only possible to say that the schedule is firm at this point in a relative sense. All designs are subject to modifications of one kind or another throughout their useful life. Sometimes the modifications are so far-reaching that it is reasonable to regard the design as a new model. From the point of view of those in the production control department who draw up the schedule each modification, however small, necessitates a critical re-assessment of the previous schedule and in most cases the issue of a new schedule taking the modifications into account. Up-dating of this kind is very important since the efficacy of the planning processes which are required when the production is actually authorised is very largely dependent upon the accuracy of the master schedule used as a basis.

Some companies are concerned only with the production of standard lines of product, and these are made either on a flow line basis or in batches which can be fitted into available capacity in an orderly sequence. In the case of flow line production the processes, once started, follow a well understood sequence and control by reference to the master schedules is relatively easy. This is because capacity demands have been analysed with care and plant and equipment provided to meet the demands. Upward variations in demand are met by the installation of new plant and equipment or by the sub-contracting of some of the additional work. In the case of sub-contract work the delivery dates required of sub-contractors can be derived from a study of the master schedules.

Much the same considerations apply to the batch production of standard lines. If demand rises it is sometimes possible to meet the contingency by decreasing the interval between the initial loading dates of batches, but this may, of course, have an adverse effect upon the rate of production of batches of other lines. There is obviously less free capacity between loadings in which to accommodate these other lines. Again, therefore; the solution may lie in the expansion of capacity or in sub-contracting.

Another factor to be taken into account in regard to the master schedule is that of method change. As experience of a method of production is gained it is inevitable that better methods will be devised. These may arise from shop floor suggestions, and the supervisor has a big part to play here, or they may be put forward by the work study officers. Whether the changes arise from these or any other sources they will if the proposals are adopted, almost certainly result in time saving. If that is the case the master schedules must be altered accordingly. Such time saving will often mean that additional equipment or sub-contracting to meet increased demand is not required. This is an aspect of increased productivity which should be the concern of all who have to do with the actual manufacturing processes on the workshop floor just as much as it is the concern of those involved in higher level production management, design, process planning or work study.

Manufacturing to Special Order

The implication here is that an order of precisely this kind has not previously been undertaken, although the class of work will almost certainly be familiar. Equally, although an exactly similar job may be undertaken in the future, there is no certitude that that will be so.

In view of these implications there is often a temptation to dispense with a master schedule and proceed directly to machine loading. Such a practice has considerable drawbacks and is not to be recommended. If it is accepted that the loading of workshops is of such paramount importance that the process should be planned, then it is essential that the whole of the work passing through should do so on a planned basis and not just that which is likely to be continuous or respective. Loading work on to producing units is a highly complex problem, and this applies to all types of work. Therefore, before detailed capacity planning, or loading, can be undertaken it is necessary that broad base or outline plans should first be prepared.

It can be argued, with some force, that scheduling is even more important with non-repeating orders than with continuous flow work. This is because in the nature of things the job which is in continuous production will eventually be sorted out into some semblance of order by mere repetition and the correction of errors. Again it is sometimes argued that non-repeating orders are in production for relatively short periods and the preliminary scheduling work is too lime consuming to be worthwhile.

These arguments are failacious. If relatively short runs of more or less unplanned work are inserted into an otherwise well planned programme the latter will soon suffer. The short-run work, being only partially planned, will almost certainly either over-run the time allocated for the longer run jobs, or will finish earlier than anticipated and cause idle time or readjustment of the long-run plans.

The difficulties of providing proper schedules for all work passing through the factory are recognised, and the reluctance of management to allocate time for short-run scheduling well understood. Basically, however, the problem is one of policy. If short-run special orders are to be accepted as a policy, then they must receive similar planning treatment to that provided for long-term jobs. If that approach is unacceptable then the sales policy should be that short-term orders are unacceptable. Where the latter policy is adopted there are frequently arguments along the lines that either accepting short-term work attracts customers with long-term work to place, or that short-term work can often be very profitable. There is an element of truth in both these views, but it is far less than the supporters of such arguments would have us believe.

The truth is that it is by no means easy to find a factory having the skills and capacity needed for short-run work. In the main those which approximately meet the need are small, often not very well managed and lack really suitable plan and labour. Those which have the skills and capacity, therefore are often approached with the htnt of bigger orders to follow. It is unwise to place too much faith in this 'sprat to catch a mackerel' approach.

That short-run orders can appear to be very profitable is true. The occasions where they really are so profitable are, however, infrequent. Merely because the income handsomely exceeds expenditure on labour, material and overheads it is often assumed that a good profit has been made. This is because the losses causes by the disruption of other work cannot easily be calculated. In most cases no such attempt is made. Not only that, but the disproportionate amount of time spent by supervisors and managers in solving the problems of the new job mean that other work suffers. The real drawback to short-run work is that it provides exactly the same problems as does long-run work in the initial stages, but there is no long-run to follow upon which the extra expenditure can be recovered. Thus policy should so far bs possible be directed to accepting either long-run or short-run work. Sometimes a mixture must be accepted, but in any one of these three cases scheduling is essential.

Scheduling and Sales

Master schedules, or subsidiary schedules derived from them, may be built up from data on the basic operations to be performed, as shown in Fig. 6.2, or they may start from the broader base of the work to be performed within different workshops or even different factories. Whatever the breakdown might be they all at providing the groundwork for later more detailed planning and permit a properly disciplined approach to questions concerning the giving of reliable delivery dates. If an inquiry is received requesting a delivery date for a given quantity of products the appropriate master schedule can be compared with the charts showing the current and forthcoming load on the factory. The comparison will immediately reveal if the demand can be met and if not what alterations to existing plans would be necessary for it to be met. If alterations are not contemplated then the comparison will enable the best possible delivery date to be determined under the circumstances.

Clearly, when the inquiry is for a quantity of a standard product the necessary schedules for comparison will already be in existance and the process of deciding a realistic delivery date will not be unduly difficult. However, when the factory undertakes special work it is not possible to make the comparison in the manner described without first preparing at least an outline schedule. Because this adds to the cost involved in preparing the estimate for quotation purposes it is often dispensed with. In consequence the delivery promise given is often very little more than an informed guess. In fairness, it should also be pointed out that when a company undertakes special work it is usually in the position, at any particular point in time, of not knowing which or how many of its outstanding quotations are going to become orders. Therefore, offering firm delivery dates can be something of a gamble. If three quotations, A, B and C, are outstanding and only A becomes an order, then the delivery promise will probably be met. If, however, all three develop into orders then one, or possibly more, will over-ruu the premises given. Despite the validity of this argument there can realiy be no question that delivery promises derived from even an outline schedule will at the very least be more realistic than are those which are not, A further point is that although schedules do take time to produce the information required for their compilation is required for the preparation of the estimate in very many cases. All that is then required is to translate it into the form needed for the schedule.

Enough has already been said about the importance of keeping delivery promises for it to be unnecessary to repeat it at this point. What must, hower, be emphasised is that it is not possible for production control to give reliable promises to sales without some form of schedule for guidance.

Working in the fashion described has also a further advantage from the viewpoint of production control. Immediately an order is received a preliminary schedule, prepared when the estimate was drawn up, can be withdrawn from file, re-examined, and modified in the light of any new relevant information, and entered on to the master schedule. Somtimes this wiil reveal that orders received in the intervening period have absorbed capacity which was not allocated when the original quotation was sent to the customer. If that is the case, produetion control can immediately advise sales and provide them with a new date. This will mean that sales will have to obtain customer approval of the revision, and sometimes that will be an unwelcome process, either to sales or the customer or both. Even so, it is better to advise the customer of the true position within a few days of receiving the order than to hope for the best and then be obliged to advise him of the revision when his expected delivery date is approaching. Provided the company has built its reputation upon keeping dates or alternatively of giving revised dates in good time, then only limited harm will be done. Obviously the ideal position is to keep to the date given in the quotation, but that is not always possible for the reasons given earlier. The company does not know which quotations will produce orders and which will not.

SCHEDULING AND PURCHASING

Reference was made in Chapter Two to some of the problems encountered by the purchasing department when it is endeavouring to play its parts in ensuring a smooth flow of materials to meet the needs of the factory.

One of the most important aspects of effective purchase control is the question of time. Time is consumed in finding and selecting sources of supply, placing and chasing orders, and in checking incoming goods. Careful preliminary scheduling provides are purchasing department with a reasonably accurate picture of what are likely to be the future production demands with a maximum margin of warning.

When preliminary schedules for quotation purposes are prepared it is possible in many instances for the purchasing department to carry out a check, if only in broad terms, of what materials are likely to be needed, how much and when. Where the sales department is able, as it often is, to give an opinion about the likelihood of obtaining the order, the purchasing department can, if it so decides, make a few preliminary investigations. These could be internal in the case of material normally held in stock. For example, it may be that certain material will be needed in three months' time if the order is received. Will stock then be adequate to meet demand and, if not, when must orders be placed to ensure delivery in time?

If the materials which might be required are not normally held in stock, the difficulties of obtaining them might be checked. If they are difficult a little deeper investigation might be required. Some at least of this work might well have been done already at the estimating stage and often further pursuit of information would not be justified. The point to be made is that the preliminary schedule provides the buyer with maximum forewarning of a possible order. Reference to sales will frequently provide some indication of the chances of the quotation being accepted and purchasing can then prepare for the work up to a certain point.

Obviously there will generally be only a few occasions when the purchasing department will actually buy material for an order not yet received. On those occasions when that risk is taken the schedule and a knowledge of the delivery date given to the customer will enable the purchasing department to advise the supplier of the dates by which material is required.

When orders are received and the tentative schedules become a part of the master schedule and are thus written into the plan for future production, they provide the purchasing department with invaluable guidance.

Clearly the schedule alone will not necessarily give the buyer all the information he needs. Practices differ from firm to firm. Some schedules, backed by a master material schedule, will give a great deal of detail and the buyer will require no further information before proceeding to order. In other cases the schedule may give only a broad outline of the stages of production. Where this is so the purchasing department will either require a detailed schedule and material list or a dated material list giving the dates by which material will be needed.

SCHEDULING AND FINANCE

In a properly managed concern it will not be the practice to accept orders or to plan production beyond the capacity of the capital available to finance the project. In the initial stages, however, consideration of the sums of money involved may well be restricted to lump sums only loosely related to time. The schedule, either tentative before receipt of the order, or firm afterwards, will show in more precise terms the points in time when production will for example, build up, peak and then decline. Hence the points will be revealed when the investment will be high and when returns from the customer may be expected. Such information is of great value to those in the company who are concerned with the problems of each flow.

SCHEDULING AND INSPECTION

Quality and reliability of the product are key factors in successful marketing. In order that the work of the inspection department may be effective it is necessary that it should be planned and integrated with the production processes.

Successful planning in this field, as in others, is firmly based upon an adequate supply of information well in advance of the point where action will be required. From the viewpoint of the inspection department the principal source of information about the anticipated forward load is provided by the production control department. Immediately an order is received it is then possible for the latter to issue master or updated schedules giving the dates proposed for the starting and finishing of the various stages of the work to be done. With this information the inspection department can begin any preliminary planning required in order to ensure that inspection facilities in term of manpower and equipment can be available when and where required.

7

Inventory Control: Overview

INTRODUCTION

The purpose of this paper is to describe a special area of production management, described in my terms of reference as "production planning", "production control" and "inventory control".

In order to define my own area of interest, I propose first to make a short review of the whole field of production management, next to show the boundaries of my own area; next again to describe this area in greater detail, and finally to tell you why I believe that this is a particularly rewarding and important part of production management.

PTODUCTION

Production is defined in the English dictionary as "the manufacture and distribution of goods". In this enormous field there is one conception which is universal. All production starts with natural materials and is concerned with the progressive change of the "state" of these materials into forms which are more highly desired by human beings.

The movements of materials through production is described as "material flow". There is an obvious analogy with, say, the flow of a fluid in system of pipes. It should be remembered however that whereas in hydraulic flow the changes of state of the fluid are mainly in respect of location or position, in material flow the changes of location are accompanied by fundamental changes in, for example, shape, weight and chemical composition.

This conception shows the way in which natural materials are progressively converted by a series of work operations into products, and it shows how we normally divide the total flow stream into "production units" specialising in different processes, or series of closely related operations. It shows also by the dotted line, that normally each production unit has a choice of source for the supply of materials. By this mechanism we obtaina potent incentive towards improvement. Each production unit attempts to improve its quality and reduce its costs; and thus obtain a larger share of the market, and each production unit attempts to make its suppliers contribute to this aim, by searching for the supplier who can provide the required quality at the minimum cost and with the most regular delivery. I mention this to show why I cannot help you with ths problem of industrial planning in its broadest aspects. In Englandwe do not—on principle—plan the material flow between factories. My experience starts with the individual factory.

ANALYSIS OF PRODUCTION

If we now examine any "production unit" or factory, and try to determine what are the tasks that have to be done to promote and sustain a required flow of materials, we find that the total task can be divided conveniently into eight main functions of groups of tasks.

By another analysis we can also observe that all tasks (and therefore functions) are normally executed in three stages. First we "plan", or decide what we are going to do, next we "do" the task, or carry out the plan, and finally we "control" the doing, by comparing achievement with the plan and "feeding-back" warnings when there are variances, so that corrective action can be taken.

If we examine the planning and controlling counterparts of each of the eight main functions, we find that most of the subjects taught in production management are included.

The analysis of production will be seen that:

1. Design is the function concerned with planning the final material state to be achieved, or in other words with planning the design of the product. The control which seeks to ensure that these plans are followed is quality control.
2. Production planning is the function concerned with planning how the product shall be made. Control is exercised by process control and maintenance. Production planning in effect creates a material flow system, or system of routes through the factory for all the materials in use.
3. Production control is concerned with planning the manner in which materials shall flow through the system. It is mainly concerned with scheduling or the fixing of start and/or finishing times for the delivery of materials and for the completion of the various work tasks specified by production planning. The control used to ensure that the plans are carried out is called progressing.
4. Inventory control is the function which plans or forecasts the future level of stocks in a business and attempts to control the stock level by comparing actual stock with the forecast, and by "feeding-back" warnings where there are variances.
5. Purchasing is the function which seeks to find the best materials at the lowest cost. It issues it plans in the

form of due-dated orders, and attempts to control performance by purchase progressing and supplier rating.

6. Marketing is the function which seeks to find customers willing and able to take the products. Its master plan is the sales forecast or programme and the appropriate control is sales eontrol.
7. Organisation is the function which attempts to plan the allocation of authority and responsibility for different work tasks to individuals, and also to plan the relationships and lines of communication between them. Establishment control is one of the methods used to see that the actual organisation matches the plans.
8. Finance is concerned with the flow of money in the business. As materials are paid for, money flows out. As products are sold money flows back in again. If we are efficient more flogs in than flows out and we make a profit or surplus. The flow of money is intimately related, but in an extremely complicated way, to the flow of materials. The accountant attempts to forecast the effect of the planned material flow on the money flow and to produce plans in the form of budgets, standard costs and cash forecasts.

The controls used to see that these plans are followed are known by such names are budgetary control, higher control and standard costing.

It should be noted that the eight names used for these functions are merely labels. They do not attempt to describe the whole job. For example the function of production control includes both planning and control, and so also does the function of production planning.

A second point: these eight functions are convenient units for study because the tasks they include are all closely related and the subjects when divided in this way can described progressively. The functions do not necessarily make good units of organisation. For example, design and quality control are not necessarily the responsibility of the same manager.

To complete this analysis of production, it is necessary to consider four other groups of subjects which must also be studied by the manager if he is to be any good.

1. Development techniques: Under this heading I include all subjects which are concerned with this scientific study and critical analysis of the enterprise with a view to its gradual development and improvement.

   One of the most important is work study, which in a very narrow sense is mainly concerned with process planning, but in a wider sense can be used in any part of production. We sometimes use special terms for the work study approach depending on the field in which it is applied: for example "Organisation and Methods", or "O" and "M" in the field of office work, and "design analysis" in the field of product design.

   Other development techniques with the same aim of critical analysis and improvement, are "operational research" and "market research".

2. Technology: All the subjects we have considered so far have a universal application to all production management. The general principles can be taught with advantage to managers in any industry. A designer, however, although he can benefit by instruction in the principles of design, will still be a poor designer unless he also knows something of the technology of his product. A production planner again can learn with advantage the principles of production planning, but will be useless unless he also had some knowledge of the technology of the processes which he plans.

   Most industrial managers have to have this dual expertise; both in management subjects and in some special technology, if they are to be successful.

3. Production economics: This subject studies the relationship between the material flow and money flow systems in production. It seeks to determine the effects of different policies in all the eight divisions of production on the cost, profit and capital tie-up in the business.

   We have recently grown out of a phase in which we believed that this relationship was simple, mechanical and mathematically exact. We now realise that is extremely complicated and very difficult to predict quantitatively.

   However, although we cannot exactly predict the quantitative relationship between material flow and money flow, we can predict the directional change in cost, profit and so on, which will tend to be induced by a given direction of change in the productton parameters. We can in effect learn how to steer the business. This new approach is reflected in the new science of cybernetics.

4. Humanistic studies: Finally the good manager must also know something about the human relations side of management. These subjects are difficult to teach, because there are few universally accepted principles and we are still at the searching stage. They are, however, probably the most important subjects of all. One has only to imagine the effect on productivity, if it were possible to promote in industry the same co-operation and enthusiasm that one finds in an average football team, to see that this is so.

PRODUCTION PLANNING

My special field in production management covers the three functions of "production planning", "production control" and "inventory control". I will now very briefly describe the ground covered by the first of these.

For efficient planning in all but the simplest of situations, it is generally necessary to divide the work progressively into divisions at a number of different levels. The levels differ only in the size of the units we are considering. In production planning there are three main levels of planning, and these have become largely formalised and have acquired special names.

1. Factory planning is concerned with the broadest possible view of how the products shall be made. It considers the division of the total material flow into processes and the provision of departments where they can be carried out. It deals with such problems as the location of the factory, the type of building, whether to have a foundry and make costings, or buy them for someone else, and so on.
2. Process planning next, takes each department in turn and considers the next smaller units of the operation and the work centre. It is concerned with such problems as routing—or the specification of the material flow path to be followed by each part—and plant layout, or the spatial relationship between work centres.
3. Operation planning finally studies the individual operations and plans how they will be tackled. It works with the units of the element and the work station. Among other subjects it includes tooling design and the planning of assembly operations.

In the past production planning was largely regulated by tradition. Certain methods of factory layout, plant layout and tooling were used in all factories without question. They formed a part of our management philosophy which outside certain mass production industries, was never questioned. Today there is a new approach which places the main emphasis on good material flow.

PRODUCTION CONTROL

Production control again can only be tackled effectively, if we approach the subject progressively at a number of levels, differing only in the size of the units considered. The principal levels are:

1. Programming which considers the major units of the products and the factory, and the plans and times at which different quantities of products small be completed.

2. Ordering considers the next smaller units of the component (or assembly) and the department. It plans the times at which materials and component must be available and issues its plans in the form of orders bearing due-dates or schedules.

3. Despatching finally deals in the smaller units again of the operation and the work centres and considers the sequence and timing of the operations required to complete orders.

At each of these levels the principal task is scheduling, or the fixing of start and/or finish dates for work tasks. A closely related technique is loading, or the comparison of load and capacity, with a view to ensuring that all the available capacity in man and machine hours is used efficiently.

Again, at each of the three levels the control used to check that achievement follows the plans, is known as progressing. Its function is to give warning of variances between actual achievement and plans.

There are a number of different systems used in "ordering", to control the release of orders. For example, orders on departments may be released by the receipt of the customer's order—as in jobbing production,—or orders may be released against a programme. There is also a system known as "stock controll", in which the release of orders is controlled by the stock level. When the stock of an item drops to a predetermined level, a new order is issued for a replacement batch. I have classified eight of these systems and will try in the courses not only to describe them, but to show where they can be used and how to choose the best combination and systems for any particular factory.

INVENTORY CONTROL

Inventory control is the function which attempts to maintain stocks at their planned levels. It has four main purposes :

1. To ensure that stock do not rise so high that all the company's capital is out of circulation.
2. To maintain the balance of the stock.
3. To maintain the accuracy of the accounts.
4. To guard against theft, depreciation and obsolescence.

The control is exercised by forecasting or planning the required stock levels at regular intervals, by counting and valuing the stock at the same intervals and by comparing the two sets of figures to find variances.

This function is also widely known as "stock control", but I prefer the present nomenclature, in order to prevent confusion with the "ordering system" in which the release of orders is controlled by the stock record. It will be realised that this type of system—stook control—does both jobs. It couples care of the inventory and control of order release.

Unfortunately "stock control" is one of the least efficient of all the ordering systems and its use for the general control of ordering is decreasing rapidly. As a result inventory control is developing into a separate system which first attempts to forecast the level of stock which will be induced by the production plans and policies, and next compares actual stocks with those forecasts or plans, so that excessive growth or depletion of stock does not arise.

THE FUTURE OF PRODUCTION

I have now briefly reviewed the whole field of production management and have described, in a little more detail, the three special functions in which my main interest lies. I must now teil you—as promised—why I consider that three functions are of particular importance to production today.

I believe they are important because I believe that the main advances in the future are going to come from improved material flow. We have already seen somethieg of the potentialities of this approach in the mass production industries and in the small number of "lines" which have been fully automated. We are now finding that exactly the same principle of putting good flow above all other considerations can also be applied with great advantage to mixed product, small quantity production. Although all eight functions are concerned in this approach, the main responsibility for promoting good flow falls on production planning and production control.

Let me give as an example, the case of a large engineering factory in France making electrical switch gear. Because this type of product is generally "special", they make an enormous variety of different products. " Nevertheless they are making many of the components by 'line production". To achicve this ideal form of material flow.

1. The divided they components into "families", such that all the components in any one "family" could be produced on the same plant in the same sequence. To obtain this division they modified many of the component designs and modified some of the processing routes.
2. They next laid out the plant for each family of components, with the plant arranged in its standard sequence of use.
3. Finally they tackled the setting-up problem and reduced all setting-up times to a matter of seconds, so that the lines could be changed frequently without loss of capacity.

In those sections of the factory which have been converted, the now make today the components they will need on assmbly tomorrow : re-set the line again tomorrow to make the same components for the following day's assembly, and so on.

There are three main advantages that can be expected from flow improvement exercises of this type :

1. A big reduction in stock: In Britain for example in the manufacturing industries alone, we have stocks totalling £ 5,000,000,000, for a net output of £15,000,000,000. In the future we will undoubtedly be able to sustain such a level of output with half this stock. By reducing the national investment in stock and releasing capital for reinvestment in new plant and equipment, we can hope for a substantial jump in productivity.

2. A reduction in indirect labour: If the flow system is complicated and inefficient, the control of material flow is extremely complicated. If the flow system is simple, control and administration are extremely simple. For example with a completely integrated line flow system, the production control task practically disappears. Providing that materials are received into the factory at the correct rate, the flow system itself automatically regulates the transfer of material and tools and the allocation of work. We can hope in the future to use a much higher proportion of our labour on productive and creative work, and a much small proportion on unproductive data processing.

3. Greater flexibility of planning: It is not uncommon in an engineering factory to find that the total machining time for a component is only 4 per cent, of the "throughput time", or time elapsed between receipt of the material and despatch of the product. In such is situation it is only possible to sustain production by forecasting what one will need for sale in, say six months' time, so that the materials can be ordered now. If the throughput time can be reduced to the same as the machining time, one can throw away the "crystal ball", and it is then possible to change designs and

production programmes very quickly without wasting large quantities of material.

You may feel that in these observations about the future, I have been prophesying and that you would prefer to hear what is being done now, rather than hear speculations about the future.

Most of my courses will in fact deal with present techniques and methods, but I hope you will allow me some latitude for prophecy, because I believe it is important to Poland. If you are going to shoot a duck you do not aim at the duck, you aim at the point where you think the duck will be when your bullet reaches it.

CONCLUSION

In conclusion may I very briefly review the contents of this paper.

First, I defined production and showed that the one universal concept which applies to all production is the concept of material flow.

Secondly, I considered the total task of promoting and sustaining material flow in a production unit; showed that this task is normally divided into eight main functions, and showed that we generally tackle each of these functions in the three stages of "planning", "doing" and "controlling".

Thirdly, I mentioned four other groups of subject which the manager must study and master, if he is to be efficient.

Fourthly, I described in a little more detail the three functions of "production planning", "production control" and "inventory control" in which my main interest lies. And finally, I speculated on the future development of production and attempted to show why I believe that these three functions are of particular importance today.

ANNEXURE 7-A

The Place of Materials in Production and Inventory Control

Introduction

What is Production ?

1. Definition; the manufacture and distribution of goods.
2. The concept of material flow.
3. The division into specialising production units.
4. Competition and the flow between production units.

Analysis of Production

1. Division of the total task of promotion and sustaining material flow into eight main functions : design; production planning; production control; marketing; purchasing; organisation; inventory control and finance.
2. The three stages in carrying out any function: planning doing and controlling.
3. Combining the two analyses finds most of the subjects taught in production management.

Complementary Subjects

1. Development techniques; research: work study; operational research; design analysis, etc.
2. Technology: Both of the product (diesel engine, wool, chemicals, etc.) and of the process (casting, forging, machining, assembly, spinning, weaving, distillation, etc.).

3. Production economics, or the relationship between decisions taken in all functions, and the money flow.
4. Humanistic studies. (Personnel functions, training, research).

Inter-Relationship Between Functions

No decision can be made in the furtherance of any one of the functions, without some effect on all the others.

Advantages of Analysis

1. Study.
2. Organisation.
3. Management philosophy.

Summary

Production Planning

1. Must be based on an AIM, which generally takes the form of product, marketing and financial policies or plans.
2. For efficiency, planning must be progressive at a series of levels, varying in the size of the units considered.
3. "Factory planning" (the first level), considers processes and departments. It is concerned with such subjects as the location of the factory, the buildings and services, the broad policy decisions re. "make or buy", the division into departments, the flow between them and the layout of departments.
4. "Process planning" (the second level), considers operations and work centres. It is concerned with such subjects as routing, plant layout, handling and the planning specification.

5. "Operation planning" (the third level), considers elements and work centres. It is concerned with such subjects as the design of tooling, the sequence of elements and the layout of work centres for manual operations.
6. At all three levels we are concerned with planning both sequence of work and the spatial relationship between the places where work is done.

Production Control

1. Must again be based on the AIM, but is further limited in scope by the decisions made in production planning.
2. For efficiency it must again be progressive.
3. "Programming" (the first level) considers the factory and the products.
4. "Ordering" (the second level) considers departments and components.
5. "Despatching" (the third level) considers operations and work centres,
6. At all three levels the task to be done is "scheduling" or the fixing of finishing and starting times for tasks.
7. A closely allied task is "loading", concerned with the roads imposed on labour and on work centres by the different plans made in scheduling.
8. "Progressing" finally is the function which compares actual achievement with the plans made in programming, ordering and despatching and "feeds back" warnings to line management when there are variances.
9. The principal parameters of production control are batch quantity, batch frequency and ordering phase.
10. There are eight main systems of ordering, used to control the release of orders onto production departments. They can be divided into "order controlled'.

(the customer's order); "stock controlled" and "programme controlled" groups.

Inventory Control

1. The function which measures the stock at regular intervals, compares it with planned levels and feeds back warning of variances.
2. The aims of inventory control are:
    1. To conserve the capital,
    2. to maintain balance,
    3. to maintain the accuracy of the accounts,
    4. to control obsolescence,
    5. to avoid theft and depreciation.
3. With "stock control" systems of order release, inventory control and production control are fully integrated.
4. With all other systems they are closely related but separate.
5. In inventory control we are mainly concerned with measuring the quantity and value of the stock, checking the balance of the stock, checking for loss, depreciation and obsolescence, and reconciliation between the "actual" to "accounting stock."
6. The term "inventory control" is often used to cover the control of all other assets, as well as stock.

The most emportant of these three functions production planning. If it is done well the other two are greatly simplified,

Summary

8

Materials' Inventory Control Checklist

GENERAL

Inventory control is a procedure by which the quantity of materials is theoretically held between predetermined limits.

Inventories themselves do not create income. They are expenses to maintain. The cost of carrying inventory is composed of several items such as:

(a) losses from depreciation, obsolescence and possible theft;

(b) interest, taxes and insurance on the investment;

(b) storage charges.

The cost of carrying inventory should be minimised, but total cost must be evaluated in the light of the risk or being short of materials.

Inventory level is affected by the following factors:

(a) effectiveness of external transportation;

(b) type of industry;

(c) extent of standardisation;

(d) extent of standardisation;

(e) seasonal variations in demand;

(f) production methods.

RECORDING INVENTORY CHANGES

In order to operate an inventory control all changes taking place in inventory levels or things affecting this level must be recorded, These are:

(a) materials received in stockroom as a result of purchase orders;

(b) materials received as a result of production orders;

(c) raw or finished materials removed from stockroom for sale or use;

(d) inventory counts taken.

The inventory control should be informed about these changes as soon as possible. An example of inventory control record is given in Figure 8.1.

SYSTEMS OF INVENTORY CONTROL

Basically there are two methods of inventory control: max-min-method and requirements-method.

MAXIMUM-MINIMUM INVENTORY CONTROL

This system requires that the following factors be determined for each material or class of material:

(a) how much of the material that is scheduled to be used or sold during the next year or the next production cycle. ("Average use line");

					Date	6/7/58	
Inventory Control Record					Reserve	35	
					Order Pt.	140	
					Ec. Lot Size	280	
Date	*Refer. No.*	*Quant. Ordered*	*Quant. Received*	*Balance on Order*	*Quant. Issued*	*Used Balance*	*Balance on Hand*
1/5							Inv. 152
1/10	784				20	20	132
1/16	801				50	70	82
1/24	893	280		280			
1/25	901				35	105	77
2/1	914				10	115	37
2/3	893		281	0			318
2/7	939				41	156	277
2/13	983				35	191	242
Card No. 1 for 1958			Part Name			Part No.	

Fig. 8.1: Example of Inventory Control Record

(b) how long it takes, on the average, from the time the purchase requisition or the manufacturing order is released until the material is delivered to the stock-room ("Lead time");

(c) how large the reserve stock should be to provide a comfortable safety factor. ("Reserve stock");

(d) what is the economic lot size to manufacture or purchase. ("Order quantity").

Figure 8.2 explains the principal relationships in stock variation.

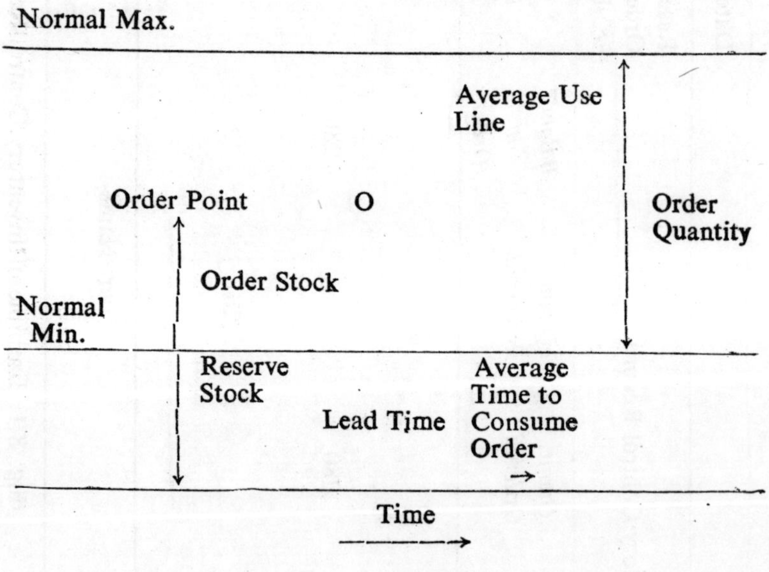

Fig. 8.2

REQUIREMENT METHOD OF INVENTORY CONTROL

This method calls for ordering of materials on the basis of requirements as specified by incoming sales orders or the sales forecast.

This requirement must be specified to cover an indicated period of time, and the quantity per delivery must be determined in each case based on the daily requirement.

ECONOMIC LOT SIZE

Some costs associated with a shop order occur once with each order. This fact calls for large orders to spread such costs over a large number of units.

Other costs depend on the investments in inventory. Small runs minimise investments in inventory and keep these costs low.

The economic lot size is the optimum compromise at which the sum of these two types of costs is minimum.

In general, the total annual cost (T) of producing a commodity is equal to the sum of the following:

(a) fixed costs (F), *i.e.* executive salaries, depreciation;

(b) unit cost (U) multiplied by annual quantity produced (Q);

(c) order costs (S) multiplied by the number of orders per year $\left(\frac{Q}{L}\right)$;

(d) carrying charges (C) multiplied by value of average inventory, which is the "minimum" stock plus one-half the lot size, (K+1/2 L) multiplied by unit cost (U).

Putting this analysis into symbols:

$$T=F+(U\times Q)+S\times\frac{Q}{L}+\left[C\times U\times(K+1/2L)\right]$$

The lot size that minimises T is found to be

$$L=\sqrt{\frac{2\times Q\times S}{U\times C}}$$

Annual quantity Q must be estimated and adjusted for present inventory and desired year-and inventory.

Order costs S are costs that vary with the number of orders and are relatively independent of size of order:

Set up costs

costing costs

planning costs

(material handling costs sometimes)

Unit costs U vary with annual quantity produced and are relatively independent of lot sizes and number of lots:

direct labour

Material

some variable burden.

Carrying costs C include all costs that vary with the size of the investment, *i.e.* inventory:

interest

taxes

insurance

obsolescence

space costs, etc.

Note: It is often difficult to determine these cost factors accurately. Several reasons may make it impractical to use economic lot sizes in actual production; or even calculate economic lot sizes:

the order itself is too small;

cost or computation may be too high;

only approximate reliability can be expected,

(difficult to foresee future needs, changes occur in demand, costs etc.);

operational policies may call for other lot sizes or other inventory levels.

BLOCK AND LOAD CONTROL

In some industries the products go through almost exactly the same operations, but unlike the continuous production which uses flow control, production must be controlled by bunches or lots. This has to be done because the products are not exactly alike. Various hybrid types of control are used in these companies; some use the expression "block" control, others "load" control, while still others do not have a specific name.

Block Control

In this form of control, orders or batches of products are assigned to "blocks" of work, usually in accordance with their due dates. In order for it to work effectively, these blocks must represent equal amounts of work in each department, and therefore equal blocks of time. All the blocks must go through the same fundamental phases of the basic process, and the production division must be departmentalised on the basis of these phases. Manufacturing capacity must be balanced between department,s for otherwise these blocks will move through different departments of different rates. As blocks of work are released, they are numbered serially, and as a rule they must be processed in this order. The progress of the blocks through the different departments can be controlled easily by reports. Differences in styles, sizes and models can be taken care of without great difficulty. Block control is well fitted in clothing and shoe factories.

The Clothing Industry

In the manufacturing of suits a "block" is usually the plant capacity of a half day, For example, if it is 200 suits, block

No. 1 containing orders of various quantities totalling 200 will start in department A in the morning and leave it for the next department at noon. When a new block or lot of suits enter a department, the foreman signs for it. The clerk crosses off each suit or order as it is finished, until every order on the block is crossed out. As a block is delivered from one department to the next. the block number is reported to the main office as cleared in that particular department. No block is cleared for any department until it is complete. A report of blocks behind schedule goes to the factory manager each day,

In the shoe industry a similar procedure is used. There are, however, more departments in this industry and there are more chances for delys because of more machines used in the processes. The control problems are therefore somewhat more difficult.

Load Control

In some industries the production control problem is one of apportioning the production time on large, expensive, fast production equipment among several varieties of almost identical products. Often the periods of time on major equipment required for particular products are rather long. Production control is largely a matter of loading the equipment.

Processing Authority

Work routing, and the forms necessary to instruct workers how to produce are more like those used in line production. The production control department seldom tells the plant how to do an operation or what operations to perform. Semi-permanent standard specifications are nearly always used to describe the results wanted from each operation. The detail instructions have to work in order to achieve these results and are in most cases decided by the foreman or group leader. Standard specifications are generally kept in specification books with loose-leaf pages. The engineering or technical department keeps the books up to date. Production control and each producing department should have complete specification books.

Producing Authority

Production in semi-process companies is either to stock or to sales order. When production is to stock, the authorisation received by production control is generally a weekly release like in flow control, while to sales order copies of sales orders act as authorisation. This holds true for both "block" and "load" control companies, although load control industries manufacture most of their products to stock.

Preparing for Production

In block control industries (clothing and shoe), the preparatory work is often quite similar to that required in order control.

Raw materials' requirements have to be computed and it may be necessary to reserve qantities for certain orders.

In the shoe industry the availablity of lasts must be checked, as must heels, laces, buckles, soles, and other accessories.

Operation lists are used but somewhat differentiy than those used in order control. They are printed because most are standardised. Figure 8.3 shows an example from the clothing industry In the shoe industry it may contain more than 100 operations.

Tags are prepared by production control. They serve to identify materials or as job tickets.

Scheduling is usually done on a department or group basis.

Load control companies manufacturing to stock usually have a daily or weekly order list arrangement to convey requests for products to the PPC department, When large pieces of equipment must be loaded, the production in most departments is directed be means of daily schedules for each key machine or piece of equipment.

Ser. No.		*Coats*		*Amount*
		Shop................		
Reg. Bx No.	Lot Block No.		Shop No.	
Customer's Name:				
Button	Model		Spring	Fall
Lined				
Pattern	Matching	Cutting	Stripe	
Edges	Seams			
Armhole		Waist Dart		
Skirt Pockets				
Outside Breast Pocket				
Inside Breast Pocket		Cash Pocket		
Centre Slit				
Sleeve Finish				
Belt				
Under Collar			Pocket No.	
Pads	Heads	Canvas Front		Sleeve

Silk	Sub Silk	B.H. Twist	Hanger		Button Thread
Buttons		Seam Piping		Neck Pads	
Keep Stripe out of Facing Edge					Date
Overcast					
Body Lining		Sleeve Lining			
Trimmer					
		(Stub Tags)			45085
	(Operation)				
	45085				
	45085				
	45085				

Fig. 8.3: A work order used in men's clothing industry
Stub tags cover every operation

Inventory in process causes some problems in load industries because there is often a lack of balance in the productive capacity of key operation machines. Large quantities of material may pile up because of the high rate of production and the lag in time between one operation and the performance of the following.

Dispatching

In block control companies the PPC department feeds orders to the initial department in accordance with the plant's approximate capacity to produce. No other dispatching is done.

In load control each key machine has a schedule showing the type and quantity of material to run and usually indicating the time of day when each type is to be run.

Progress Control

In block control, the progress of production is reported daily or twice a day to production control. In most companies the job-tags act as reporting media.

In load control, the schedules sent out for key operations provide spaces for recording the quantities produced as each run is finished. The schedules are returned daily after production to the central office and serve as a report on output.

TOWARDS BETTER INVENTORY MANAGEMENT

There are problems faced by Indian industry, in the area of inventory management. The constraints imposed by these problems, on company practices and efforts at inventory planning and control, have also been reviewed, based on the IFMR Survey.

Are these constraints and handicaps to be accepted as the causes and compulsions for the general atmosphere of managerial helplessness, in matters concerning inventories? Or are they to be viewed as opportunities for organised management to prove its mettle?

This section advocates a shift from apparent non-management to better management, as the essential step to contain the adverse effects of these constraints and handicaps, and to improve the overall performance of the organisation. It calls for the re-shaping, rather than the rejection, of the well-known tools and techniques of inventory management, to suit the Indian context.

The approaches to better managemeut have been considered in four phases:

1, General aspects,
2. Organisational aspects,
3. Operational aspects, and
4. Evaluation aspects.

The inventory management goal can be interpreted as the avoidance of over-investment or under-investment in inventories, as an essential step in improving profitability, Determination of the right level of investment in inventories; consistent with maintenance of smooth flow of production and prompt customer services, is the crux of inventory management. Leslie R. Howard narrates the case of a company that was under considerable pressure bankers and creditors, because its inventories were found to be very high and very badly deployed. Remedial action involved raising the inadequate inventory levels for some items, and redueing those of others, which were held in excess. The over-all reduction in inventory investment, thus, does not imply uniform cuts in all items but involves a rational examination of the excess or shortfall in the inventory holding of each item, consistent with the expected activity and sales of the company, and carrying out the necessary correction. This calls for a departure from the blanket approach that is often adopted in selection of inventory control measures, and the adoption of an enquiring approach to assess the nature and action needs of each significant inventory component.

General Aspects

Attitudinal change is found to be the essential and the first requirement, for introduction of purposive inventory management, in many cases. Certain hard convictions and sacred beliefs may need to be changed, and this concerns the tactical steps to provide the right perspective, and wear out resistance to the introduction of new systems. This management of change has to be necessarily initiated and sustained by top management.

Let us look at some of the reactions to the IFMR Survey. One response indicates that the company's inventory is so composed that it does not warrant any computation of inventory carrying cost, purchase order costs and stock-out costs. If this stand is the outcome of a careful examination of the company's inventoried items and their special characteristics, it is a studied judgement and has to be accepted as an operative dictum. But this could well be a broad opinion that has gone untested, has come to stay and, as a result, the organisation might have opted for a long-term. sub-normal path of operations.

Another response concedes that the company has not, so far, felt the need for E.O.Q. computations or the calculation of relevant costs for inventory control. In this case, these are arguments against the application of the techniques, and the field is open for initiation of worthwhile action. The company might have already paid a sizable price for the delay in this regard, in terms of avoidable costs and reduced profits.

On the plea that, owning to the small size of its business, inventory control has not posed any serious problems, another organisation has mentioned that it has been following the rule of thumb. Whether the relevance of inventory control is to be established in relation to the size of the organisation, is the larger issue involved here. Inadequacies in inventory planning and control are bound to cut into profits, whether the company is larger or small. The mechanics of control may, of course, depend upon size and other consideration,

Striking a firm note, one respondent declares that Materials Management does not really make any profit, either by planned purchase of material, or control of inventory. It is further asserted that it is not possible to quantify savings, if any, made by it. This is an emphatic contradiction of the general proposition that effective inventory management will enhance the profitability of the organisation, in a variety of ways. It will take quite an amount of organisation and effort to erase this misplaced not on, of the gains of rational Materia's Management.

The top management's close involvement is fundamental to any concerted approach to scientific or rational inventory management. The three-fold objectives of increasing net earnings, improving customer service and sales, and reducing working assets, have direct relevance to the management of inventories, which constitute a dominant investment segment. Through policy guidelines and appropriate procedures, for continuous review of material productivity and optimality of investment in inventory, the top-management should create an organisational awareness of the high priority assigned to result-oriented materials and inventory management. Only then will the aims and practices at the operational levels get suitably attuned.

A common failing, often evident, is the *ad hoc* or piecemeal approach to the attainment of the objectives mentioned above. Management attention might, at one time, be devoted to an organised attack on excess inventory. Subsequently, the focus might shift to improving customer service, and this might cause the inventories to rise again. Then there might be a switch-over to a spate of profit improvement activities, with the emphasis on volume increases, and in this race against time, inventory administration may receive low priority. These abrupt directional shifts have to be consciously avoided, and the need for simultaneous and balanced attention to all three objectives, has to be emphasised. Many organisations have experienced the three-stage drifts from a period of concerted action programmes for inventory reduction, to one of satisfaction and complacency, followed by unregulated inventory growth, in the span of a decade or so. This is far from the desired goal of sustained efficiency and economy in inventory administration.

The science of inventory management has grown into a highly technical and mathematically rich field of knowledge. Operations Researchers and Management Science specialists have presented a wide range of mathematical models, to suit different inventory situations. These scholarly contributions have come from researchers in industrially advanced countries, where the environmental infra-structural and operational conditions are very different from those obtaining in India. The assumptions underlying these mathematical models may not have ready relevance to our conditions. The basic concepts and principles, however, have universal validity, and we should address ourselves to the task of evolving models that would suit our needs. By its very nature, inventory management has to reckon with a vast array of numbers, whether one is concerned with inventory levels, lead time implications, economic procurement volume or batch quantities, costs or prices, and these inevitably need to be studied and interpreted in mathematical terms. It merits mention that frequent attempts are being made by some of our practitioners in materials and inventory management, to interpret and resolve inventory problems mathematically, and these appear in some of our professional journals. However, they seem to receive inadequate attention from a great majority of these intimately associated with inventory management.

Government policies and procedures, transport bottlenecks, power shortages and several other factors have been often mentioned as impediments to 'the application of scientific techniques to inventory management. But the Survey has shown that some of the companies have been fairly successful in tackling, if not altogether eliminating, many of thess impediments, and their success can be traced to their better organisational and managerial abilities.

Organisational Aspects

Inventory managemenl embraces all major functional areas in an organisation. In the conventionat set-up, the Purchase and Stores departments share the procurement and storage responsibilities for raw materials and stores, the Production department has purview ever work-in-process while the Marketing department takes responsibility for finished goods inventories. Thus, different classes of inventories receive routine attention from different departments/functional areas. Very often, these involve little more than custodial responsibilities for the concerned departments, with due attention for documentation and procedures for storage and releases. These departments tend to operate as separate units, each within its allotted domain. The essential features of coordination and high level direction and control will, in such cases, be found missing. It is not unusual to find these departments understaffed or inadequately equipped, even to attend to these routine operations. Materials Management obviously needs to be elevated to a much higher status in the hierarchical ladder of the organisations.

In some organisations, Materials Management has developed as a subsidiary function of one of the major functions like Finance or Production. A degree of coordination and centralised direction is anticipated in the set-up, but this is seldom achieved. The concerned major functions are heavily pre-occupied with their own specialised fields, and accord secondary importance to the line function of Materials Management, looking up to them for effective support and guidance. The intended objective of high level coordination and direction of Materials Management thus falls short of achievement.

There are interesting instances where the Stores department is regarded as the depository of recalcitrant, unwanted personnel who have been found misfits in other departments. Whereas, in terms of knowledge of materials and components, ability to assess sources of supplies, the sense of trusteeship in respect of inventories held, and administrative calibre, stores personnel have in fact to match high standards, if they are to be effective. Careful attention to staffing, training and development of personnel in the Materials Management area is a must. The Materials Management function has to be upgraded considerably in terms of recognition, status and the quality of its personnel. The Chief of the Materials function, should be on a par with the Heads of the other major functions such as, Production, Marketing, Personnel and Finance. This will be an important step towards consistent and coordinated high level direction and effective control.

Among the findings of the Survey, there is mention that, out of the 48 respondent organisations only 2 have adopted the integrated approach to Materials Management. Consider the following common sets of procedures for materials acquisition and storage. (A) indents, (B) scrutinises, (C) approves the items, quantities and prices, (D) gives financial concurrence, (E) places the purchase orders, and (F) receives the items, inspects, stocks and issues for consumption. With such a division and sequential sharing of step and action, who can be held responsible for excessive inventories, if any, that have got accumulated? Who has the ultimate responsibility for effective inventory control? The pattern of organisation fails to provide a satisfactory answer to these questions. It is an instance of everybody's responsibility being nobody's responsibility. Any approach to integrated Materials Management endeavours to design the organisational structure in a manner that the total responsibility for inventory planning and control is assigned to a senior executive, heading the Materials Management function, and he directs decisions and actions at all phases of materials movement.

One of respondent organisations is planning a switch-over to the integrated concept, and after due consideration of the company's needs, has evolved an amended Organisation Model. The pattern of organisation, now in existence, is shown in Fig. 8.4 and the proposed version in Fig. 8.5.

The proposed model intends to bring, under the purview of the Materials Manager, the total inventory of the organisation, including raw materials, work-in-process and finished goods. At the operational phase, the activities coming under the direction of the Materials Manager will include.

(a) Materials planning and inventory control

(b) Materials purchase

(c) Materials receipt, storage and issue

(d) Production planning and control

(e) Ancillary development and sub-contracting

(f) Import substitution and indigenisation

(g) Systems development and computerisation.

While the above pattern cannot be recommended as a standard model, for all situations, the underlying objective of integrated coordination has significant relevance to all organisations desirous of rationalising] their Materials Management efforts. Each can incorporate the concept of integration in its organisational structure, keeping in view its operations, processes and products.

OPERATIONAL ASPECTS

Materials Codification

Materials codification can be said to be the foundation on which the whole edifice of inventory control is built up particularly in large organisations. With thousands of items entering into inventories, it becomes difficult to use long

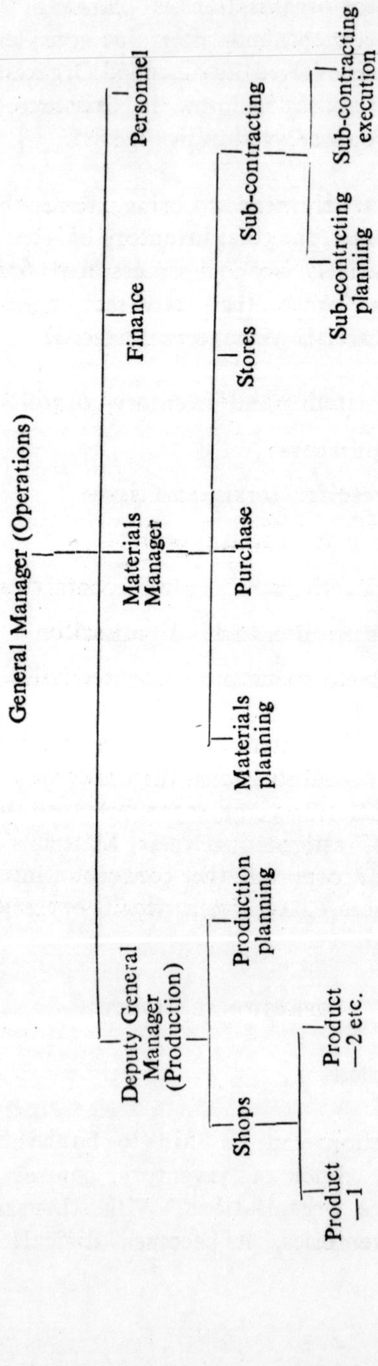

Fig. 8.4: Existing organisational structure

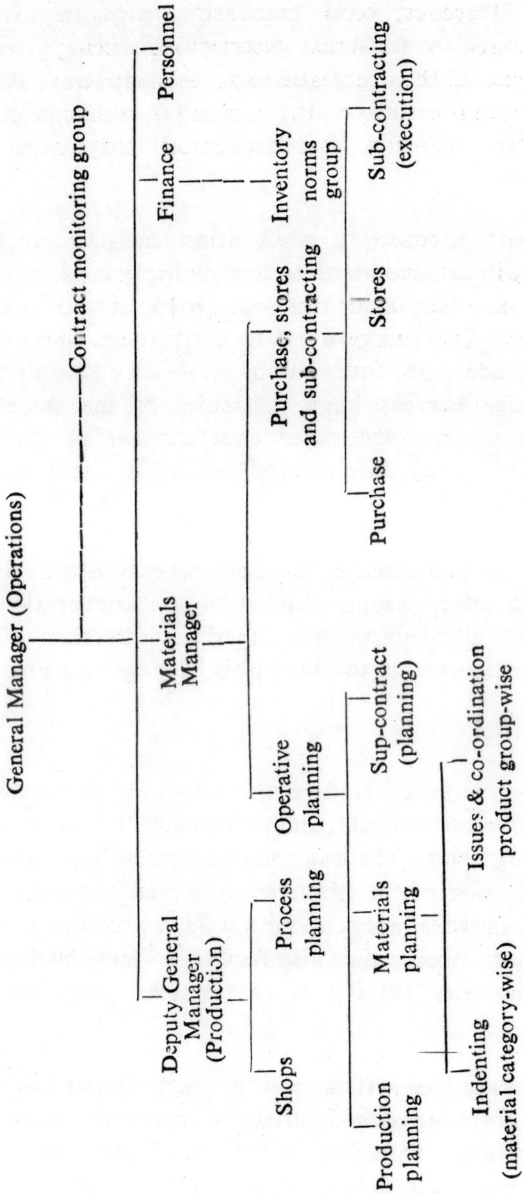

Fig. 8.5: Proposed organisational structure

descriptions. Moreover, code numbering helps in averting confusion caused by different descriptions being given by different people in the organisation to the same item. Besides facilitating data processing on the computers, codification also helps in variety reduction, standardisation indigenisation of imported items.

Half-hearted approach to codification can do more harm than good. It is not uncommon to find multiple code numbers given for the same item under the same group, as well as under different groups. This can give rise to a situation where there is a stock-out under one code, based on which rush purchases might be made, whereas huge quantities of the same item might be lying under some other code number in the same or some other group. This creates avoidable imbalances in inventory levels.

Designing and introduction of a comprehensive and effective material codification system requires active cooperation and participation of all departments, under the direction of competent senior executive, in the Materials Management area.

Variety Reduction

Proliferation of varieties hinders the adoption of an effective policy of stock replenishment, and perpetuates the accumulation of slow moving items. The lesser the number of items and their varieties, the greater is the effectiveness of planning and control. Reduction in varieties brings about a welcome reduction in the total minimum stock, and also facilitates bulk buying, with resultant economies. Talking of the benefits, one respondent says:

The benefits of the system can be immediately felt in the stores, in the form of reduced variety of materials, consequent reduction in storage handling, and lesser paper work in the Material Control and Purchase departments. Monetary benefits like reduced inventory costs can be further felt, after disposing of the materials classified as redundant.

Among the variety reduction techniques employed, the respondent mentions:

(a) Ordering and Classification
(b) A-B-C Analysis
(c) Design Unification
(d) Preferred Numbers.

Standardisation

There are substantial imports of capital goods and spares, and these come different foreign sources. This gives rise to the problem of multiple specifications; the answer to it is standardisation, with the help of International Standards Organisation Foreign collaboration efforts, involving transfer of technology, should also take into consideration the standardisation and interchangeability aspects.

One respondent organisation, which has made considerable progress in its programme of standardisation, lists the gains in following words:

Standardisation not only saves the direct measurable cost of parts, material, etc., but also has several other advantages, as given below:

(a) maximum utilisation of available standard parts, standard tooling and material.
(b) uniformity in drawing, planning manufacturing and inspection processes.
(c) simplified training.
(d) engineering time saved.
(e) material selection made right, even for the first fix.
(f) with simplified communication and coordination among departments, greater understanding can be created

among them so that no misunderstanding arises while designing, drafting, planning, manufacturing, inspection, assembly and testing of the final product.

Standardisation ensures practical application of the principles of Engineering and Technology, in the most economical and effective manner. The manufacture of the same parts like bushes, bearing covers, etc., of different machines requires the same type of machining operations, and such items can be manufactured as stok order items, so that they can be drawn, for the individual machines. This reduces process time and paper work in Production Planning. Further, the manufacture of increased batch quantity reduces the set-up time and increases the productivity. Coordination between the various departments will be more effective. With the reduced cost, the quality of the product can be well maintained. As such, there is hardly any industry to which will not accrue the benefit of standardisation, if it accepts. Organised standardisation is a part of modern industrialisation, which will help in efficient working.

The above company has prepared the following standards files, based on local puichase specifications:

(a) Standards Parts file

(b) Basic Standards file

(c) Raw Materials file

(d) Tool and Equipment file

(e) Consumable Goods file

(f) Foundary Materials file

(g) Index for Cost Numbers

It has yet to extend standardisation to the following fields:

(a) Product standards

(b) Planning standards

(c) Time Study standards

(d) Process standards

(e) Maintenance and service standards

(f) Industrial Safety standards

(g) Handling and Storing standards

(h) Packing standards

(i) Workshop standards

(j) Control standards.

Forecasting Materials Requirement

While uncertainties of supply, government policies and procedures, transport delays, etc., render forecasting exercises difficult, they cannot be dubbed wholly responsible for the inept forecasting of materials requirement in many organisations. With better internal organisation, with the introduction of the concept of integration of materials management, and with adequate base by way of codification and standardisation, forecasting abilities can be considerably improved, and the implications of external interferences on lead time, prices, etc.,can be assessed through appropriate sensitivity analysis. In quite a few instances, there will be scope for application of sophisticated techniques such as Exponential Smoothing and Regression Analysis.

Some among the repondent organisations have mentioned that they employ the Materials Requirement Planning System (MRP). MRP is a tool to project the requirements for various components and parts, from the master schedule, by a level-by-level explosion of the bill of materials. Gross requirements thus arrived at are netted against available inventory, and orders on hand, for each component, at that level. Project-wise non-repeatable materials, A and B classes of materials, as also V and E categories of C class materials are brought under the MRP system. All materials classified under MRP hould be planned and indented for, only on the basis of actual requirement. The rest of the materials, coming under the stock control category, will be planned and indented for on the basis of pre-determined levels.

Cost Perspectives

The Survey revealed a general lack of cost perspective in inventory management. Assorted physical and quantitative controls over inventory levels are in vogue, but these are not framed on the objective of minimising the total cost of having plus not having inventories. While the argument of unreliability of supplies, unpredictable lead time variations, etc., can be valid in respect of some items of materials, there must be a good many others, which can lend themselves to reasonably good estimates of deliveries, lead times, etc. Computations on relevant costs, and ordering and holding levels, should be possible with respect to these normal items. The selective application of these methods and techniques has considerable scope, which many organisations seem to overlook.

The following illustration shows the method of identifying relevant inventory carrying costs.

Elements of cost	*Variable Fixed*	*Cost in terms of Percentage*
1. Cost of investment in inventories (opportunity cost/interest)	V	16.00
2. Stationery	V	1.00
3. Insurance	V	1.50
4. Pilferage	V	1.00
5. Obsolescence and deterioration	V	1.50
6. Wages of daily employees	V	2.00
Total Variable Cost		23.00

7. Salaries and wages of monthly rated employees of stores	F	2.50
8. Salaries of stores account section	F	0.50
Total Cost		26.00

First, the elements of costs, relating to inventory carrying, are identified. These elements are segregated into variable and fixed costs, applying the criterion that variable costs increase/decrease as the level of inventory increases/decreases.

An illustration of the computation of purchase order cost follows:

In the first place, the number of purchate orders released during the accounting year is collected as given below:

Value per Purchase Order	*Number of Purchase Orders*
Rs. 1,50,000 and above	129
Rs. 10,000 and above but below Rs. 1,50,000	829
Blow Rs. 10,000	4,273
Total	5,231

The next step is, to collect element-wise expenses incurred during the same period, in connection with processing and releasing of purchase orders.

Element of expenses	*Fixed expences*	*Common variable expenses*	*Total expenses*
	Rs.	Rs.	Rs.
1. Postage	—	12,000	12,000
2. Trunk call charges	—	15,000	15,000
3. Telegrams and telex	—	35,000	35,000
4. T.A. & D.A. for purchase follow-up	—	60,000	60,000
5. Stationery	—	20,000	20,000
6. Salaries of personnel of purchase department	3,72,000	—	3,72,000
7. Salaries of personnel giving financial concurrence for purchase proposals	60,000	—	60,000
Total	4,32,000	1,42,000	5,74,000

The following calculations give the cost of placing a purchase order.

(i) Fixed cost per purchase order $= \text{Rs.} \frac{4,32,000}{5,231} = \text{Rs. } 83$

(ii) Variable cost per purchase order $= \text{Rs.} \frac{1,42,000}{5,231} = \text{Rs. } 27$

(iii) Total cost purchase order $= \text{Rs. } 83 + \text{Rs. } 27 = \text{Rs. } 110$

(iv) Expenses incurred on advertisement, during the same period, for purchase orders whose value was

Rs. 1,50,000 and above, was Rs. 60,000. The number of purchase orders in this category was 129. Therefore, the identifiable variable cost per purchase order in this category is: Rs. $= \frac{60,000}{129} =$ Rs. 465

The relevant cost for inventory control is Rs. 27, which is the variable cost per purchase order of the value below Rs. 1,50,000. In the case of purchase orders whose value is Rs. 1,50,000 and above per purchase order, the relevant cost is Rs. 27+Rs. 465=Rs. 492.

The fixed cost is time dependent, and does not vary with the variation in the number of purchase orders, in the short-run, and therefore, is considered as sunk cost.

Lead Time Compression

For effective inventory control, administrative and procurement lead times have to be analysed, and the procedures properly streamlined, to minimise administrative lead time. Procurement lead time is, to a certain extent, beyond the control of the unit level management, but it can be shortened by effective purchase follow up.

The longer the lead time, the larger is the safety stock required, resulting in excess investment in inventories. Therefore, endeavour should be made to cut down the lead time to the barest minimum.

It is often pointed out that in organisations where financial concurrence is a must for purchase proposals, lot of avoidable dealy is experienced in getting concurrence from the Finance department. It is better to have, in such organisations, written guidelines to give financial concurrence for all purchase proposals.

Spare Parts Control

In order to use all available foreign exchange, which is scarce, orders have to be placed often with suppliers in different countries. This results in equipment of differing specifications being used in an industry, and, even within one organisation. This inevitably leads to larger requirements of spares.

The solution to these problems can only be found in greater indigenous capability for both equipment and spares. This is necessarily a long-term goal. Even in the short-term, steps need to be taken to encourage indigenous suppliers of spares. For this purpose, drawings of the equipment components should be purchased, together with the equipment, and supplied to indigenous manufactures. The smaller local manufacturers will also require to be assisted with production and quality control services.

It has to be borne in mind that for certain special items, the material composition and its metallurgical properties are crucial. Without these, more drawings will not be adequate. It is encouraging to find that some respondent organisations have recognised these requirements, and are initiating necessary research and developmental action.

From the stand-point of the individual organisation, the inventory level of spare parts depends, very much, upon the confidence level of the maintenance crew, and where the tendency is to play safe, the spares inventory piles up fast, in the guise of insurance spares.

With regard to insurance spares, in each organisation, a specialised inter-disciplinary team consisting of operating, maintenance, and industrial engineers, as well as inventory analysts, should examine the question in detail, and advise the concerned management as to where risks must be covered and where a calculated risk can be taken, in respect of break-down and possible stock-out. Otherwise, every time a new imported equipment is to be installed and commissioned, it will start with a handicap of heavy initial spares. Where stock-outs are taken as major indicators of an inefficient procurement plan, the tendency is to play safe, since inventory carrying costs will at best be latent costs, which do not come into prominence.

A ceiling of spares holding, of 5 per cent of the original plant and equipment cost, is desirable.

Economic Order Quantity

In industry, there is a tendency to discard E.O.Q., as an outdated concept, with the plea that the cost estimates can never be exact, and will vary from one item to another, depending upon sources and other factors. One respondent remarks:

> For Indian conditions, exercise of E.O.Q., will only be theoretical. Bottlenecks of transport, power disruption, political instability, labour unrest throw any prefixed delivery schedules out of gear.

Several difficulties have been cited by the respondent organisations, in their effort to implement the E.O.Q. system. Cost-sensitivity analysis will indicate that even if the E.O.Q. is modified, taking into account practical considerations, the total cost increase will be marginal in many cases. This introduces the concept of E.O.Q. Range. That is, in the total cost curve, the curve is flat near the E.O.Q. indicating that ordering a little more or a little less than E.O.Q. will cause only marginal changes in the total cost of ordering and holding. In practice, 25 per cent above or below E.O.Q. will not make much of a difference to the total cost.

Some respondent organisations using the Materials Requirement Planning (MRP) system have stated that the E.O.Q. is not applicable in their situation. It is to be noted that MRP is a planning technique, whereas the E.O.Q. is used to aid purchasing. In such situations, Aggregate Inventory Control

Technique (AICT) can be used. The E.O.Q. formula, as applied to individual items, indicates a desired optimum condition for each item. However, when it is applied to all the items produced in a given machine group, it may reveal certain unpleasant surprises. Fven though the sum of all the E.O.Qs. of individual items should add up to the least total cost in an inventory, model, it may really call for larger investments in inventory, or increase in total number of orders to be processed by the existing clerical force, or mcrease in the space required for storing, as compared to the requirement under the Aggregate Inventory Control Approach. In other words, the E.O.Q., applied to a total system may have an off-setting effect, if we do not investigate the effects of the individual E.O.Q. on the total system.

The technique for handling E.O.Qs. in aggregate, and dealing with problems of constants in calculating the E.O.Q. was developed as a special project for the American Production and Inventory Control Society, at Chicago in 1963. It is known as the Aggregate Inventory Control Technique (AICT)* or the Lot-size Inventory Management Interpolation Technique (LIMIT)**

Norms

With a view to avoiding losses in storage/handling, and to obviate any chance of pilferage wastage, organisations should fix consumption norms of various materials, and check the actual consumption, periodically, with the norms to locate cases of excessive consumption.

For purposes of controlling the overall level of inventories. organisations should establish norms as ceilings for inventory

*Brown R.G., Aggregate Inventory Management, APICS annual Conference Proceedings, pp. 111-119, 1962.

**Harty J.D., Plosse G.W., and Wight O.W., Management of Lot-size Inventories, A Special Education and Research, Report of the American Production and Inventory Control Society, Chicago, Illinois, 1963.

holdings. Any manager conscious of the importance of Materials Management will view this control mechanism, as an effective means for taking remedial steps, as and when necessary.

Data Processing

With the advancement of computer science, and with the growth and sophistication in software packages and support, many leading organisations are using computers for inventory control applications. However, in several organisations, computer use for inventory control is not effective. It is not unusual to get statements several weeks after transactions: Lots of snags exist, such as inability to ensure correct and timely inputs to the computers. Sometimes accounting procedures, which are predominantly 'audit' oriented, come in the way of timely output of statements.

Further, in many organisations using computers, the area of application is only inventory accounting and not inventory control.

Another serious failing is improper documentation. The Production and Maintenance departments are usually too busy to maintain records of stores, spares and other materials. When an indent is sent, a good part of the justification form is either left blank, or filled up with approximate figures. How precise and accurate the procurement decisions can be, with such information gaps, is anybody's guess. It is very essential to establish the most vital link between consumption, stocks, dues-in, working stocks, safety stocks, purchase order, receipts and inspection for atleast A and B class items, without which inventory control will not be effective. This vital link has to be, preferably, established on the computer, which takes the shape of a "data bank" inventory control, for retrieval of the requisite information, for making analysis and for taking quick decisions.

EVALUATION ASPECTS

To assess whether steps taken by the organisation, for improved inventory management, yield the desired results consistently, it is necessary to develop reliable performance indicators for periodic review. Traditional indicators, like the number of months' holdings in stores as compared to budgeted consumption, or number of months' finished goods in ventory vis-a-vis budgeted sales, serve as broad, over-all signals for bankers or top management, but are not adequate for functional managers, who are more concerned with sorting out day-to-day problems of co-ordination in respect of materials, and matching production or despatch schedules with commitments. So, in addition to traditional inventory reports, there is the felt need to develop a further set indicators, which relate organisational goals to departmental goals. Among the relevant performance indicators could be:

(a) The number of material hold-ups, in each major group of materials, for each major production centre, for the different products being manufactured. This indicator helps in reviewing the availability status of materials. Every month or quarter, this should show a declining trend, till shops get the confidence that they are getting material, in accordance with marketing plan.

(b) The number and value of high value items, in each major groups of materials, in stores, for more than 3 months, 6 months and 12 months, without movement. This indicator will help in questioning and correcting the assumptions underlying materials planning and indenting.

(c) For work-in-process, the review of actual production cycle time, for major sub-assemblies or component codes. Year after year, this indicator should show a lowering trend, in the background of a sound inventory management system.

(d) The number of incomplete work orders, more than 6 months, or one year old, in shops.

(e) For finished goods inventory, the statistical time delay analysis, between the time a despatchable unit is handed over, and the same is invoiced.

A textile unit, which had responded to the Survey, has the following set of reports for periodic review:

(a) Godown Stores Inventory

(b) Unserviceable items laying in Stores .

(c) Pending Indents

(d) Baling Consumption

(e) Sizing Material Consumption

(f) Rejected goods not lifted by suppliers

(g) Bills passed

(h) Memo received against urgent indents

(i) Packing materials balance

(j) Stores consumed in excess of monentary ceiling

(k) Cash Purchases

(l) Statement of pending orders.

Another organisation, engaged in the manufacture of steel castings and industrial machinery, reviews performance on the basis of the following information, provided by its computer wing.

(a) Activity Report, once a fortnight, showing opening stock, receipt, issue and closing balances in both quantities and values.

(b) Stock Status Reports for standard items for purchase, for material planning and placement of orders. This statement gives the opening balance, receipts, issues, closing balance, minimum and maximum levels, order quantity and order level.

(c) Marketing Stock Statement, item-wise; showing stock quantity, rate, value, dated of last receipt and date of last issue.

(d) Department-wise and work-order-wise monthly consumption statement.

(e) Variance in consumption and price of major inputs.

(f) Perpetual Inventory Verification Statement and Summary.

(g) Non-moving Stock Statement.

(h) Material-wise Annual Consumption Statement.

(i) Annual Activity Statement of Imported Items.

(j) Mobility Analysis.

(k) Vendor Analysis.

The nature of review data and the periodicity of review will depend on the specific needs of the organisation. But it is essential that as much of involvement as possible, from senior and top management levels, is ensured during the performance reviews.

DO'S AND DONT'S

Given below are some do's and dont's for Materials Managers. This is not a comprehensive checklist. The intention is to draw attention to certain significant action steps.

1. In the case of A-class items, plan on increasing the frequency of purchase orders, to reduce the capital tied-up at any given time, inventories.
2. In the case of regular consumption A-class items, try to cover as many items as possible, by six-monthly or annual contracts, with scheduled deliveries.
3. For the remaining A-class items (not covered by contracts) develop and revise more often, ordering quantities, reorder points and safety stocks.
4. Follow the normal procedure of an automatic replenishment system, in respect of stock items where there is a regular pattern of consumption.

5. Ensure that the purchase department should not blindly believe that their major duty is to convert every indent into a purchase order, without even reviewing the quantity at the time of processing the purchase requisition.
6. Group all C-class items like electricals, hardwares, paints, in individual groups and order in lots, preferably from one or two vendors. This saves ordering work and cuts transportation costs. In addition, because of the inclusion of several items in one order, each order becomes large enough for the vendors to make concessions and give discounts.
7. For the ordering of C-class items, use a combination of the review period system and the two-bin system.
8. Do the V-E-D analysis for classification of maintenance spares, denoting the essentiality of stocking spares.
9. Do the S-D-E Analysis where certain items are scarce, and decide on the purchasing strategy.
10. Do the H-M-L analysis for keeping control over consumption at departmental level, and for deciding the frequency of physical verification,
11. Do a movement analysis of the items, namely, the F-S-N and X-Y-Z analysis, to reduce obsolescence.
12. Give preference to suppliers who have demonstrated a low rate of rejections in materials supply, and delivery schedule reliability.
13. Arrange production programme in such a way that, to the extent possible, all customer orders are processed in the sequence committed. This means giving higher importance to customer satisfaction, in the matter of delivery, If the customer does not want manufactured goods, as per schedule try to charge ground rent and interest on investment in finished goods inventory.
14. Do keep a record of vatiations in lead time for A and B class and other critical items. It helps in determining order levels and safety stock.

15. For A-class items, use fixed-review-period and variable-quantity system. But single-order staggered-delivery system will be ideal, wherever possible.
16. For B-class items, use either fixed-quantity-ordering and variable-cycle system or maximum-minimum stock system. Single order-staggered devivery system may also be used, wherever possible.
17. Do not take inventory levels for granted, once these are fixed since factors like lead time and consumption rates are dynamic. The levels must be revised, as and when changes occur in any one or all of the factors.
18. To guard against the danger of obsolescence, as a general practice, purchase high value sub-delivery items strictly in accordance with Material Requirement Planning System.

SUMMARY

There is, today, a felt need for a break-through in the areas of materials codification, establishment of data banks choice application of inventory control procedures, techniques and systems, and high level review and evaluation of inventory management effectiveness. Quite a few organisations have made good progress in integrating and rationalising inventory management practices. But a large many are yet to start on the rewarding path.

9

Dispatching and Follow-up in Order Control

DISPATCHING

The Planning and scheduling sections of the production control department work out all the control functions prior to their actual use in the shop. Dispatching is the release of the orders to the producing departments. It is also concerned with directing movements of work and making reports in accordance with the routing, scheduling and other planning already done.

Because of the complexity in job-lot shops, dispatching has to be organised with a more or less flexible plan. Emergency jobs may appear at any time and if the control department assumes a rigid attitude, it will be only a matter of time until the shop will have to get along without a P.P.C. department.

In most shops it is necessary to have to dispatcher in close contact with the foreman and the shop conditions. The usual method is to have the dispatcher located in the foreman's office, or preferably in a separate small room in the centre of the area to be served. Since dispatching is a service function to the shop executives, the dispatcher must be the type of individual who can give certain directions to the workers without interfering with prerogatives or prestige of the foreman.

THE RESPONSIBILITIES OF THE DISPATCHER

1. The issuance of orders to move material from place to place as necessary to complete the scheduled operations.
2. The issuance of tool orders to the tool crib, which will reserve all the tools required for the order.
3. The control of the movement of raw material to the first operation.
4. The control of the delivery of finished goods to the finished goods store.
5. To meet all required scheduled dates and to ask for extensions with reasons for delay stated.
6. To report at frequent intervals to the central office concerning the progress and delays of the various jobs in process and waiting to be processed.
7. To post job tickets or job orders on the dispatch board and to dispatch the various jobs through the most economical process and machines available when the material is ready.
8. To eliminate unnecessary set-up costs by combining orders going through the same operation whenever time or economic lot considerations will permit.
9. To contact the time study department if the piece rate for an operation is not determined or has to be corrected.

THE CHIEF DISPATCHER

In a plant using a number of dispatch stations it is usually necessary to have a chief dispatcher to supervise the group. He work from the central production control office and coordinates the various stations and reviews recommendations for changes.

A successful dispatcher must like to work with small integrated details, must be accurate and above all firm but cooperative.

Figure 9.1 shows in chart form the ordinary routine of a typical dispatcher's office. This routine will vary somewhat with the system used but in general this is the type of control exercised in most plants.

PROGRESS REPORTS

The easiest part of production control is to make up and pass out orders. It is far more difficult to adjust or replan because of any number of reasons interfere with the perfect working of plans and thereby in most cases result in less production than was planned.

The dispatch offices are the eyes and the ears of centralised production control. As was mentioned under point 6, they receive information concerning production and report to the central office.

This information is received in several ways:

Job tickets furnish information as to the time operations take and the quantity of items turned out.

Move orders are turned in by truckers to indicate that the material has been moved. Usually the time also is recorded.

Inspection and scrap reports after the material have passed certain worh stations, information about how many good parts and how many rejects and possible reasons for them.

Verbal reports from foremen or others are emergency supplements to the regular reports.

Manufacturing Order

Part—A	Part—B	Part—C	Part—D	Part—E	Part—F

Routine for Parts A,B,C,D, and E similar to that for Part F

Route Sheet		
Part No.	Stores Issue Order	Authorises stores to deliver material to operation 1
Material		
Op 1	Total Order	Advises tool room to collect tools for Op. 1 ready for man
Op. 2		
Op. 3	Job Order	Instructs man to proceed with Op. 1, records time taken on job
Op. 4		
Routine for Ops. 2, 3, 4, same as for Op. 1	Time Ticket	Stamped with workers beginning and ending time on operation
	Inspection Order	Instructs inspector to examine and report work "good" and "bad" on Op. 1
Job Orders Displayed on Dispatching Racks	Move Order	Instructs move man to deliver from Op. 1 to Op. 2
Mach. 31 March, 32		

Reports made to planning dept. when "Route Sheets" are not kept by dispatcher.

Material ready—deplicate of "Stores Issue Order" sent to planning dept. to signal material is ready and waiting at first operation.	*Operation completed*—"Job Order" filled out with time taken on the operation signals planning dept. that first operation is completed.	*Quantity and Quality*—"Inspection Report" attached to "Job Order" signals the number of pieces good and bad from operation one. Replacement orders issued if necessary.

Fig. 9.1: Sequence of Dispatching Operations

Reports of operation completion are generally posted to the production control department, copy of the shop order or to the schedule board or chart. It is now possible to compare the time when the job was completed with the time when it should have been completed. Comparisons show where delays have occured and where revisions in schedules need to be made.

Figure 9.2 shows a form for reporting discrepancies. Such a report gives everyone concerned the knowledge on which to base corrective action.

Progress reports also supply information on the status of orders so that inquiries from the sales department can be answered. Ths report forms themselves are often passed on to the accounting department and to the payroll department.

REPLANNING AND RESCHEDULING

It is rather normal in production control that replanning and rescheduling take more of the work than initial planning and scheduling. Most of the changes are caused by numerous small interferences in production. Fewer, but more extensive, by the sales department.

Following is a list of some of the major causes :

1. Customers occasionally want products made differently after orders have been placed and production started.
2. Improvements in design and methods.
3. Worker absenteeism and variability in output.
4. Material not up to standard.
5. Large quantities of an item fail to pass inspection.
6. Shifts in priorities among orders.

Whenever changes in plans are made, they must be incorporated into the production papers.

Figure 9.3 shows a rework order which is almost as complete as a new work order.

Description of Item	Scheduled for Completion	Actual Completion	Status	Status Week Ago	Items Behind Sched.	Sch. Week	Sch, Month

Issued by . . . .   Date . . . .

Fig. 9.2: Schedule versus Actual Performance

Quantity	Part Name	Product and Rework No.		Part or Tool No.
Purchase Order No.	Purchase Reg. No.	Receiving Record No.	Date	From Dept.
Source Eng. change shop	Responsibility	Vendor	Charges	Vendor approves Vendor disap- proves
Reasons for Rework			Sketch	
Routing Oper. No. Dept. Station	Rework Operation			Time Set up Piece
Authorised Signatures	Debt. Date		Authorised Signature	
Inspector			Inspection Report after Rework	
Product Engineering		Number of Pieces	Inspector Tester	Date

Product Control		Accepted Reworked Scrapped	
Manufacturing Eng.			
To be filled in by Stockroom		By Part Control	For Cost Dept. Use only
Quan. Issued Credit Account Posted Stores Record Storekeeper	Store Stamp Quan. Recd. Debit Account	Stamp	
Rework Order			No. 27317

Fig. 9.3: Rework Order

EXPEDITERS

Some companies use "expediters", "follow-up men" or "stock chasers", whose primary job is to push orders. Where production control is highly centralised there should be little need for them.

In decentralised companies expediters are used in parts-producing departments. They keep selected orders moving and do not attempt to speed up production in general. Orders to be pushed are those which were accepted by the sales department on the basis of quick delivery and those which have fallen so far behind schedule that it is necessary to give them special attention to get them out.

Some companies attach expediters to specific departments where it is most likely that delays will occur. They work very closely with the dispatchers.

SUMMARY

The production planning and control department is sometimes called the nervous system of a factory. It plans in detail all the activities necessary to carry out production and coordinates the work of all departments in the plant. In order to get a view of all the stops involved, it may help to review the steps involved.

Figure 9.4 shows in diagramatic from the control technique on individual orders.

DRAWINGS AND IDENTIFICATION SYSTEMS

Identification systems are necessary for all materials at all stages in manufacture. Whatever system is used, it must be flexible in the sense that it must provide for new items to be added and old ones to be cancelled without creating confusion.

1. Drawing Identification

Drawings are basic to production control. They are usually the most important source of information to production control and to the plant. Often the drawing number itself serves as the identification number for the item shown on the drawing. Such identification numbers are used continually in the work of production control.

A. Drawing Numbers

Drawing numbers may be unclassified or classified.

Unclassified numbers assigned to drawings can only serve the purpose of identification. The numbers are assigned consecutively to drawings as they are made up.

A drawing card file is necessary and the drawing number and title must be recorded on the card. Usually an additional file arranged according to part name is necessary for cross reference.

Classified systems attempt to assign numbers to drawings in such a way that the number indicates the nature of the items shown on the drawing.

In all classification systems the identification number is made up of two or more sections of which at least one is coded.

Example:

Drawing number:	350241	
indicating:	35	Electric motor
	02	220VAC
	41	Housing
Coding:	000000	

Production Control

Individual Orders Technique of Planning	Analysis of Product	Technique of Control
1. Note kind of material 2. Note grade and quantity. 3. Determine quantities required for order. 4. Ascertain availability of material. 5. Make reservations of available stock. 6. Requisition material not in stock. 7. Prepare material move orders.	Material Unit Material Multiplied by Quantities on Order	1. Watch delivery of purchase material. 2. Release material orders at proper time.
1. Use machine analyses to: (a) plan best method of processing; (b) plan tools and fixtures required. 2. Determine time allowances. 3. Plan best sequences of operations. 4. Schedule machine loads. 5. Prepare work orders and time cards for each operation.	Machine Processes Time of Operation= Quantity on Order X Time per Unit	1. Release tool and fixture orders as required. 2. Observe actual operation times. 3. Check actual with scheduled loading. 4. Release work orders and time cards at scheduled times.

1. Specify inspection standards. 2. Plan assemblies and subassemblies. 3. Prepare inspection orders. 4. Schedule due dates on each operation on each part, or lot, and assembly. 5. Schedule due dates for whole order.	Work in Process Lost of Single Parts Sub-Assemblies Assemblies Final Inspection	1. Check quantity passing inspection. 2. Order replacements as required. 3. Release inspection orders when job is ready. 4. Observe and record completion of operations. 5. Check actual with scheduled progress of each lot or part. 6. Observe that scheduled dates are kept.

Fig. 9.4: Diagram Production Control Technique

	No. of Machine	Oct.	Nov.	Dec.	Jan.	Feb.	March
Mills for casings	1						Z
Blade millers	12						Z
Vert. B. millers	11						Z
Drill presses	4						Z
Milling machines	2						Z
Lucas B. mills	1					Z	
H.B. mills	1	Z	Z			Z	
Lathes	1					Z	
Lathes for shafts	1	Z			Z		
Blade grinders	3						Z
Grinders	1	Z	Z	Z	Z		

Note: Above chart is based on 100 per cent. running capacity.

Fig. 9.4-A: A Gantt chart used in a machine shop. Light lines indicate portion of month machines will be utilised. Heavy lines indicate monthly work loads. Months in which no work is scheduled are indicated by the letter "*Z*".

00 ↓ 99 } General product code

00 ↓ 99 } Specification code

00 ↓ 99 } Consecutive numbering of parts

HANDICAPS OF CLASSIFICATION SYSTEMS

1. Assign unlike numbers to similar items.
2. System is static.
3. Conflict between numbering of common parts and specific products containing such parts.
4. Lack of understanding may reduce its value.

B. Drawing Record Index

Regardless of the system of numbering an index of drawings must be kept. It services the purpose of :

1. Finding part description if drawing number is known.
2. Finding drawing number if part description is known,

The index card or form should also give the following information :

1. The date when drawing becomes effective.
2. If it is a replacement; the number of the drawing it supersedes.
3. Number of other drawings where the part appears.

C. Drawing Changes

If a drawing is charged (part redesigned):

Old number is retained if new item is completely interchangeable with the old.

New number is made if not interchangeable.

Increases or decreases of the number of uses of a part should be noted on drawing record of uses, but does not necessitate new drawing number.

Drawing record index, parts lists and operation lists must be changed when design is revised.

2. Raw Materials Identification

Raw material identification is usually combined with classfication.

Basis for the classification is generally the material from which the item is made.

Numerical system usually favoured. Six digits or more are common. The coding may give information about :

Kind of material.

Form or shape.

Chemical composition, size, etc.

3. Product Identification

Where drawing of parts exists, the drawing number is used as the part number.

For other parts the basis for classification is the use of the part or its type.

Semi-finished parts that are temporarily stored can be treated as raw materials for identification purposes and given code numbers in the system used for raw materials.

4. Supplies Identification

Large companies usually find it necessary to set up record cards to control inventory of supplies.

Classification system tied in with raw material identification system is usually used.

5. Classification Based on Account

Effective control of inventories usually require that there be an account for each classification of materials.

Account numbers, when classified according to commodity and/or material can easily be an integral part of the materials and product identification system.

6. Physical Identification of Materials

Few materials are self-identifying and they must be identified by some marking or tagging.

There are several possible solutions:

Metal parts may be numbered by

moulding

stamping or

etching

Steel rods and sheet metals may be painted on edge with different colours. Storage ins, location or container may be marked to identify the whole lot.

APPENDIX 9-A

Conditions Necessary for Supply Munagement Improvement: A Summary

Government policymakers and other responsible public officials in developing countries must recognize the growing importance of supply management because of its direct impact on the cost, effectiveness and progress development. They must be prepared to confront the problems developing countries face in meeting their supply and equipment needs. Some of the major problems common to developing countries include the following :

(a) The increasing cost of materials and equipment generated by world-wide inflation and other economic factors;

(b) The substantial dependence by developing countries upon imports in the absence of resources and capability to manufacture locally most of their material and equipment needs;

(c) Long delivery lead times and other delays in the supply processes consequent upon the dependence on imports; and

(d) The shortage of personnel with the requisite training, experience and skills to support high standards of performance.

A new approach to supply management that can bring about cost reduction and improve performance has been emphasized. There is a critical need for leadership from the top, cooperation by user agencies and competent management and operations by supply personnel. This need can be met by:

(a) sound policies and clearly defined objectives and plans;

(b) efficient performance guided by sound standards of operations and mateeials budgets; and

(c) well-motivated attitudes toward supply management.

The objectives, plans, standards, budgets and attitudes must be continually evaluated, revised and improved throughout the government to assure success. The conditions necessary for the success of supply management suggested by several technical experts may be outlined as follows:

(a) Government formulates policy to provide guidance on supply objectives, plans and programmes;

(b) Development planning processes recognize and incorporate supply management factors;

(c) Supply management is integrated with all government operations and its principles understood throughout the government;

(d) Realistic supply-management objectives are set to provide improved customer service at the lowest feasible costs in line with government objectives;

(e) Budgets are established for operating the supply-management function to provide for efficient performanee; actual expenditures must balance with the operating budget;

(f) Specifications and materials standards are established and updated;

(g) Purchases are made at prices consistent with the lowest ultimate cost of purchase, usage and storage;

(h) Inventory investment is in line with both lowest carrying cost and government-wide service policy;

(i) Realistic cost reduction goals are set to reduce the financial burdens of the government;

(j) Management controls and exception reporting are established for all major activities representative of functional operations;

(k) Suppliers, carriers and other contractors are properly chosen and each fairly treated;

(l) Supply managers establish in coorperation with systems analysts a programme for integration and, where applicable, computerisation of major activities;

(m) Inventory policies are established and utilized to provide more emphasis on highvalue items and less emphasis on low-value items;

(n) Transportation rates are the lowest allowable and each rate is reviewed for reduction;

(o) Obsolute and surplus materials are reviewed for disposal on a periodic basis;

(p) Scrap and waste are disposal of by the most economic means, including sales;

(q) All purchase orders are properly and accurately prepared within 24 hours of placement of order;

(r) Alternate sources of supply for critical items are available to satisfy requisitions with the least delay;

(s) All claims are processed within legal limits;

(t) A quality-control inspector visits a specified number of major suppliers per year;

(u) Procedures and instructions are written, approved and reviewed on a collective basis;

(v) Records are up to date and accurate;

(w) User departments provide feedback on supply problems as they occur and fully participate in their solution;

(x) Training programmes are established for all personnel; both local and foreign resources should be fully utilized;

(y) Employee performance is reviewed at least once each year and compensation is commensurate with performance;

(z) Employee motivation and morale are maintained at a high level.

Although the conditions outlined above may be difficult to achieve, they provide a target toward which public officials should strive in order to assure economy and effectiveness in government operations through improved supply management systems and practices.

TYPICAL COMPUTER-SUPPORTED INTEGRATED SYSTEMS IN SUPPLY MANAGEMENT

An integrated physical resources system might include the following applications:

Catalogue of Physical Resources

This computerized index usually is built on a coding and scheme, which numbers and describes each item of supplies, materials, parts, equipment, furniture, fixtures, buildings and structure and parcels of property. Sometimes purchased or contracted services such as maintenance and consultant work are include units of included in this catalogue. Other typical items of information measure, references to specifications, vendor sources, ordering quantity and cycle and other related data. This catalogue, when printed from the computer file is the basis for requisitions, inventory contract administration and other procedures.

Agency Orders and Requisitions

This application of the computer can encompass automatic approval for funds and encumbering budgetary accounts. Requisitioned items can also be grouped by warehouse location to facilitate stock picking and delivery from inventory or grouped by buying cycle for quantity purchases at lower prices, or usage for inventory and purchase projections.

Purchasing and Contract Administration

This application usually involves building a computer file of sources of supply and vendors. Requisitions or orders from agencies and departments can also be grouped by item, buying cycle or otherwise totalled for purposes of purchasing or contracting. The computer can print out purchase orders or tenders for bids to suppliers. If contracts are let, the computer can check bids and issue purchase orders. On construction or other large projects, the computer can also be used for project control and progress payments as predetermined phases are completed. This application can also be integrated with the budgetary and expenditure accounting system.

Inventory Control

This application maintains a file and produces reports on the receipts, issues and onhand-balances of inventory items. Such records can be maintained on a government—wide basis even though inventories are maintained at many locations. Recorder points and quantities can be established on the basis of minimum/maximum limits for each item, or "economic ordering quantities" (EOQ) can be computed, based on usage, cost of carrying the inventory item and other factors in a predetermined formula. Issues from inventory to agencies can be linked to the budgetary and expenditure accounting system. These four foregoing applications—(a), (b), (c) and (d)—have proven practical when designed as an integrated system. However, such a system can be further expanded by including the following applications.

Motor Vehicle Maintenance and Cost Accounting

All vehicles, whether operated as a central motor pool or assigned to agencies, can be scheduled for maintenance and replacement and accounted for by computer. This involves maintaining a file on each vehicle with such data as make, model, use. distances and hours operated, dates of service and repair, gasoline and oil consumed. This application automatically pinpoints vehicles that are underutilized or too costly to retain, and also provides reports for scheduling and controlling maintenance. The costs of vehicles can also be linked to the budgetary and accounting system and charged back to using agencies, if assigned from a central motor pool.

Equipment and Furniture Inventory

This application is an example of a less complex way to train staff and promote government-wide acceptance of the computer. It involves tagging each item of equipment and furniture with a numbered metal plate or sticker, and recording its catalogue number and description location and the person responsible for it. As such items are purchased they are added to the file, and as they are destroyed or sold they are detailed. Periodically, the computer inventory records are checked with the physical location of the item.

Building, Structures, Land and Resources Inventories

Many governments, have either fragmented or no records on the property they own. The computer makes it possible to consolidate all such records.

Summary

The advantages derived from computer applications in supply management may include the following:

(a) Uniform administration and control of physical property in all agencies and ministries of the government;

(b) Fewer inventory locations and lower inventory levels, resulting in considerable savings;

(c) A catalogue of property held facilitates standardization and inhibits acquisition of poor quality or overpriced items;

(d) Suppliers can be paid more promptly, resulting in discounts and more favourable contract terms;

(e) Savings in duplicate agency record-keeping and personnel;

(f) Savings by quantity purchases, and

(g) Capability and confidence established to justify the use of revolving funds to finance central services.

SPECIMEN PROMOTION EXAMINATION REQUIREMENTS

Open Competitive Examination for Entry into the Grade of Storeman

1. Language test (1 1/2 hours)—An essay paper testing narrative, descriptive and expository writing and legibility.
2. Figuring test (1 1/2 hours)—A paper testing ability to carry out simple calculations in addition subtraction, multiplication and division problems. Decimal operations, simple averages and percentages.
3. General test (2 hours)—A paper testing general intelligence and ability to differentiate between things.

Promotion Examination Requirements Storekeeper Grade II te Storekeeper Grade I

Store Warehouse and Stockyard Layout

(a) Layout of bins, racks and shelves in a detail issue storehouse.

(b) Layout of free stocks in a bulk issue storehouse or stockyard.

(c) Bin, rack, shelf and stock-location systems.

Receiving Goods and Putting to Stock

(a) Day book or goods inwards book.

(b) Case, crate and carton opening.

(c) Identification and checking.

(d) Receipt documentation.

(e) Placing in bins or on shelves or racks.

(f) Types of stocking for bulk goods both in the storehouse and in the stockyard.

(g) Discrepancy or damage action.

Care and Preservation

Must be able to answer questions relating to;

(a) Climatic and other factors affecting goods held in store.

(b) Toxic and dangerous goods including explosive and radioactive materials.

(c) Materials used in preservation.

(d) Materials used for the removal of preservatives.

Issuing

Must be able to answer questions relating to:

(a) Identification and selection.

(b) Packing and packaging, and packaging materials.

(c) Issue documentation.

Recording Transaction

Must be able to answer questions relating to:

(a) Tally cards, bin cards, stock record cards and simple ledgers.

(b) Tow-bin stock control system.

(c) Determination of obsolescence.

(d) Stock-taking.

Promotion Examination Requirements Storekeeper Grade I to Stores Officer

Must be able to answer questions relating to the promotion examination from the level of storekeeper grade II to storekeeper grade I and in addition must be able to answer questions on the subjects listed below:

Store Warehouse and Stockyard Layout

(a) Location of bins, racks and shelves.

(b) Pallet racking and pallet stocking:

(c) Bin location systems.

(d) Free stocking location systems.

Security

(a) Perimeter secutiry.

(b) Internal security.

(c) Fire security.

(d) Gate control and checking.

Care and Preservation

(a) The handling and storage of toxic and dangerous goods, includina explosives and radioactive materials.

(b) Refrigeration and cold rooms.

(c) The handling of industrial gases and medical gases.

(d) The cause and effect of spontaneous combustion.

(e) Inflammable storage and its construction.

(f) Explosive magazines.

Stock Control

(a) Stock control systems.

(b) Lead times.

Mechanical Handling

(a) Platform trucks, warehouse trucks, sack barrows.

(b) Lift trucks and pallets.

(c) Cranes and hoists.

(d) Hooks and slings.

(e) Gravity roller and nonpowered conveyors.

(f) Powered conveyors.

(g) Levers, rollers, case-opening tools, case-closing tools, banking machines.

Promotion Examination Requirements—Stores Officer to Assistant Supply Officer

Must be able to answer questions relating to the promotion examination from the level of storekeeper grade I to stores officer and in addition must be able to answer questions on the subjects listed below:

Accounting

(a) Unallocated stores accounting.

(b) Allocated stores accounting.

Stock Control

(a) Dues in (orders placed).

(b) Dues out (allocations).

(c) Economic order levels.

(d) Economic order quantities.

(e) Physical stock balances.

(f) Free stock balances.

Purchasing

(a) Purchasing principles.

(b) Indenting procedure.

(c) Supplier evaluation.

Assistant Supply Officer to Supply Officer

Must be able to answer questions relating to the promotion examination from the level of stores officer to assistant supply officer and in addition must be able to answer questions on the subjects listed below:

Purchasing

(a) Carriage of goods by sea, air, road and rail.

(b) Shipping documentation with particular reference to documents required for importing goods.

(c) Customs and port clearance procedures.

(d) Marine insurance.

Management

(a) Principles of management

(b) Elementary organization and methods.

(c) Communication-issue of instructions.

(d) Job evaluation.

(e) Job specification.

(f) Preparation of reports.

(g) Personnel records.

List of Known National Associations Concerned with Purchasing and Supply Management Training

Country/geographic Area	*Name of Association*	*Address*
1	*2*	*3*
Argentina	Association Argentina de Compradores	Tucuman 141-6 Piso "O" Buenos Aires
Australia	Institute of Purchasing and Supply Management	P.O. Box 75 Burwood, 3125
Austria	Arbeitsgemeinschaft Einkauf, Osterreichisches Produktivitatszentrum	Hohenstaufengassc 3, A-1014 Wien
Belgium	Association Belge des Chefs d'AP provisionnement	112 Rue de Treves B-1040 Bruxelles
Canada	Purchasing Management Association of Canada	80 Richmond Street West Toronto, Ontario M5H 2A4
Chile	Association Chilena de Jefes de Compras	Casilla 161-D Santiago
Denmark	Danske Indkobschefers Landsforening	Charlottenlundvej 26 DK-2900 Hellerup, Copenhagen
Finland	Suomen Materiaalitaloudellinen Yhdistys	Akkuteollisuus Oy, PL 22 02610 Kilo
France	Compagnie des Dirigeants d'Approvisionnement et Acheteurs de France	8 Rue du Conservatoire 75009 Paris
	Association pour le Perfectionnement des Approvisionnements dans les Services Publiques	2 Rue du Roule 75001, Paris

(*Contd.*)

1	2	3
Germany, Federal Republic	Bundesverband Materialwirtschaft Einkauf e.V.	600 Frankfurt/Main 70 Waidmannstrasse 25
India	National Association of Materials Management	Cecil-Court, 5th floor Landsdowne Road, Apollo Bunder, Bombay I
Israel	Irgun Menahaley Aspaka B' Israel	6 Sderot David Hamclech P.O. Box 16524 Tel Aviv.
Italy	Associazione Degle Approvvigionatori e Compratori Italiani	Viale Ranzoni 17 20149 Milano
Japan	Japan Materials Management Association	Terashima Building, K, 2-Chome Hon-cho, Nihimbashi Chuo-ku, Tokyo
Mexico	Confederacion Mexicana de Asociaciones de Ejecutivos de Compras y Abastecimiento, A.C.	Ave. Oaxaca No. 13 Mexico 7, D.F.
Netherlands	Nederlandse Vereniging voor Inkoop-Efficiency	Parkstraat 18 Den Haag
New Zealand	New Zealand Institute of purchasing and Supply	P.O. Box 3590 Wellington
Norway	Norsk Innkjopslederforbund	Trondheimsvn 80 Oslo 5
Philippines	Purchasing Associatian of the Philippines	Suite 403-A, Campos Rueda Bldg. Tindalo Street, P.O. Box 1876 MCC, Makati, Rizal

Portugal	Associacao Portuguesa dos Chefes de Aprovisionamento e de Compras	Alameda das Linhas de Torres 201-3—Dt.° Lisboa 5
South Africa	Institute of Purchasing, South Africa	P.O. Box 35 495, Northcliff Transvaal, 2115
Sweden	Svenska Inkopsledares Forening	Artellerigatan 8 nb S-114 Stockholm
Switzerland	Schweizerische Einkaufer-Vereinigung	Postfach 87 CH-5001, Aaurau
United Kingdom	Institute of Purchasing and Supply	Work House Westminister Bridge Road London SEl 7UT
United States of America	National Association of Purchasing	11 Park Place New York, N.Y. 10007
	National Institute of Governmental Parchasing.	Suite 922 Connecticut Ave. N.W. Washington, D.C. 20036

APPENDIX 9-B

Guidelines for Creating Position Caders in Materials Management

Supply personnel policies differ from Country to country in accordance with local purchasing and supply practices and procedures. Therefore, it would be unrealistic to propose in this study one personnel system to be applied to different situations. Outlined in this chapter are braod guidelines that could be adopted in developing job descriptions to meet different requirements. The guidelines are in two parts;

(a) a broad description of typical supply management duties in different functional categories;

(b) a specimen scheme of service for supply personnel in outline, with two supporting tables.

A. Broad Description of Supply Management Duties by Functional Category

1. Direction

(a) Sets policy guidelines, plans in broad outline the efficient ues of manpower, equipment, facilities and finances;

(b) Controls the activies of the organization in accordance with the formulated plans and policies;

(c) Establishes and maintains an organizational structure through which undertakings can be effectively controlled and operated; and

(d) Develops financial policies and exercises general control over cost.

2. Contract Administration

(a) Develops and documents routine policies, procedures records, forms inspection and acceptance criteria for contract administration;

(b) Establishes standards, classification and guidelines for specifications, scope of work and performance of contracts;

(c) Conducts contract drafting and negotiation;

(d) Administers procedures for the selection of vendors and contractors;

(e) Monitors progress reporting on all contracts; and

(f) Audits and approves certification for payment of all agreed-upon contracts;

3. Purchasing

(a) Receives and reviews all requisitions from different agencies for materials, supplies and equipment and other services, provided that the money to pay for such requisitions is available;

(b) Authorizes delivery from central stores and warehouses or negotiates buying or purchasing of requisitioned items if they are out of stock;

(c) Issues purchase orders to vendors to deliver above requisitioned items or to replenish central stores and warehouse stocks, according to specifications and catalogue description and in conformance with terms of delivery of applicable contracts; and

(d) Establishes and maintains usage records and other data upon which to base ordering and delivery schedules and cycles.

4. Specifications and Cataloguing

(a) Drafts commodity and item classifications, codes and related descriptions;

(b) Develops specifications and descriptions of material, supplies and equipment in conjunction with using agency personnel, and obtains their approval of such specifications and descriptions;

(c) Compiles and distributes catalogues to all concerned agencies for all equipment, materials, supplies and contractual services ordered and used on a repetitive basis; and

(d) Reviews needs for equipment, material, supplies and services and relates these needs to new products.

5. Inspection

(a) Establishes, manages and enforces a programme of quality and performance control for all purchases and contracts for materials, supplies and property;

(b) Develops and documents the results of such inspections, including standards, specifications, performance measurements, completion schedules and other criteria; and

(c) Makes inspections, laboratory and other tests; counts and measures, and makes other needed evaluation to insure efficiency and effectiveness of the supply operations.

6. Stores Operations

(a) Receives, stores and issues tools, merchandise, equipment and other goods against demand notes, vouchers or other documents, and notes damage or deficiencies;

(b) Enters details of goods received in storeroom ledgers or on record cards;

(c) Ensures that goods are placed in the correct position in stores, marking them with identifying data as required;

(d) Issues stok and makes requisitiöns for replacement according to instructions or own initiative; and

(e) Periodically checks stocks against stock records and submits reports.

7. Shipping and Receiving

(a) Controls or participates in the dispatch or receipt of goods and keeps records of shipments made: examines particulars of goods to be dispatched;

(b) Studies schedules and cost tables and decides upon the best method of transportation;

(c) Arranges assembly to goods and ensures that they are correctly addressed and ready for dispatch;

(d) Makes out dispatch notes and attends to such matters as insurance, custom clearance, routing and delivery; and

(e) Checks incoming goods against bills of lading, vouchers and other documents; notes damages or deficiencies and arranges delivery to appropriate pesons.

B. Scheme of Service to Create a Cadre of Supply Personnel in Government

The purpose of the scheme is to insure that suitably qualified and interested staff are available and will be attracted into supply work in the various branches and sectors of the government. It is also concerned with the proper training and development of supply personnel. It provides for the establishment of a supply and stores inspectorate to centrally staff, direct and control supply functions in the government. The inspectorate is to be headed by a director who should also be the chief adviser to the government on all supply matters including supply personnel and training policies. Essentially, the scheme seeks to upgrade the responsibility and authority of supply management through the unification and standardization of the policy and procedures relating to the functions, staffing and training in that field of activity.

The structure of the supply staff below the Director is as follows:

Principal supply officer

Chief supply officer

Senior supply officer

Supply officer

Assistant supply officer

Stores officer

Storekeeper grade I

Storekeeper grade II

Storeman

(Required functions to be indicated.)

The grading of each post should be based on the degree of financial resposibility assigned to it, as well as its relative importance in terms of job content. Appendix Chart 9A outlines relevnt qualification requirements at different grade levels and posts within the scheme. Annex. II outlines specimen promotion examination requirements.

APPENDIX CHART-9A

Specimen Job and Qualification Requirements at Different Grade Levels

Grade and Level of Responsibility	*Qualification and Experience*
1	*2*
(*a*) *Principal Supply Officer*: Responsibility: (i) to be deputy director of supplies, responsible for coordinating all or some of the major supply functions; or (ii) to be in charge of the supply organization of a major depaprtment or sector	Should have a university degree or equivalent qualification in business management, and recognized qualifications in purchasing or supply or materials handling. Must have at least ten years experience in a government purchasing or supply organization. Must have extensive knowledge and some experience of; purchasing; stock control; transport of goods by road, rail, sea and air; customs procedures and port clearance; classification and coding; stores and stockyard layout; care and maintenance; preservation and packing; materials handling; identification; verification and stocktaking; security distrihution; documentation; control of staff and job description; unallocated and allocated stores accounting; and EDP appreciation.

(*Contd.*)

1	2
(*b*) *Chief Supply Officer* Responsibility: (i) to be in charge of a sectoral or departmental supply organization; (ii) to be in charge of a group of supply functions in a central supply organization; or (iii) to be deputy director of supplies	As for principal supply officer, but the qualification in business management is not required and experience in a government purchasing or supply organization should be at least ten years.
(*c*) *Senior Supply Officer* Responsibility: (i) to be in charge of one or two major supply functions within a large organization; or (ii) to be in charge of a small departmental supply unit.	Should have recognized qualifications in purchasing or supply and must have at least eight years experience in a government purchasing or supply organization. Experince should include specialization in at least two major functional areas as well as a general working knowledge of the remaining functions in supply management.
(*d*) *Supply Officer* Responsibility: Normally supervised by a senior or chief supply officer: (i) to be in charge of a section with two or more units of work within a major function; or	Should have r gnized qualifications in purchasing or supply and r t have at leastfive years experience in a governmen purchasing or supply organization. Experience should include specialization in at least

(ii) to be in charge of a branch (headquarters or outstation) of a large departmental or sectoral supply organizatiou.	one major functional area as well as a general working knowledge of the remaining functions in supply managem
(*e*) ***Assistant Supply Officer***	
Responsibility· Normally supervised by a supply officer and supervises two or more storekeepers (i) to be in charge of one unit of work in a section; or (ii) to be in charge of branch stores.	Same as for (d), but should have at least three years experience in a government purchasing or supply organization. Experience should include at least one functional specialization and as much general background as possible of supply work.
(*f*) ***Stores Officer***	
Responsibiiity: Same as for assistant supply officer but to be more often assigned to storekeeping functions.	Should have successful completed a storekeeping course provided by the local institute of management or public administration. Should a storekeeping certificate of a suitable institute or an equivalent associate membership grade. Must have knowledge and considerable experience of stores and stockyard layout; identifying and checking stores on receipt; locating stores: putting to stock; care and preservation of stores; materials handling; receipt and issue of documentation.
(*g*) ***Storekeeper Grade I***	
Responsibility: Normally supervised by an assistant supply officer or stores officer to take charge	Qualificalion as above (f); Must have knowledge and experience of Store and stockyard layout; receiving into

(*Contd.*)

1	2
sections of storekeeping work and related clerical processes.	store; putting to stock; issuing receipt and issue documentation; care and preservation of stores, Must be able to maintain allocated bin cards or ledgers.
(*h*) *Storekeeper Grade II*	
Responsibility: Same as for storekeeper grade I but requires more supervision.	Should have successfully completed a storekeeping course provided by the local institute of management or public administration. Must have at least one year experience as storeman. Must have the same knowledge. though not the degree of experience of those functions referred to in (g). Must be able to maintain allocated bin cards or ledgers.
(*i*) *Storeman*	
Responsibility: To be supervised by a storekeeper to carry out subclerical and simple manipulative duties.	Vacancies should be advertised annually and candidates invited to apply to sit a written examination in accordance with requirement "A" The examination will be followed by an interview before a board of the supply and stores inspectorate and successful candidates will be required to undergo a four-week course in supply and stores training before beingposted to a stores depot.

APPENDIX CHART-9 B

Supply Management Specimen Structure of Posts—Single-function System

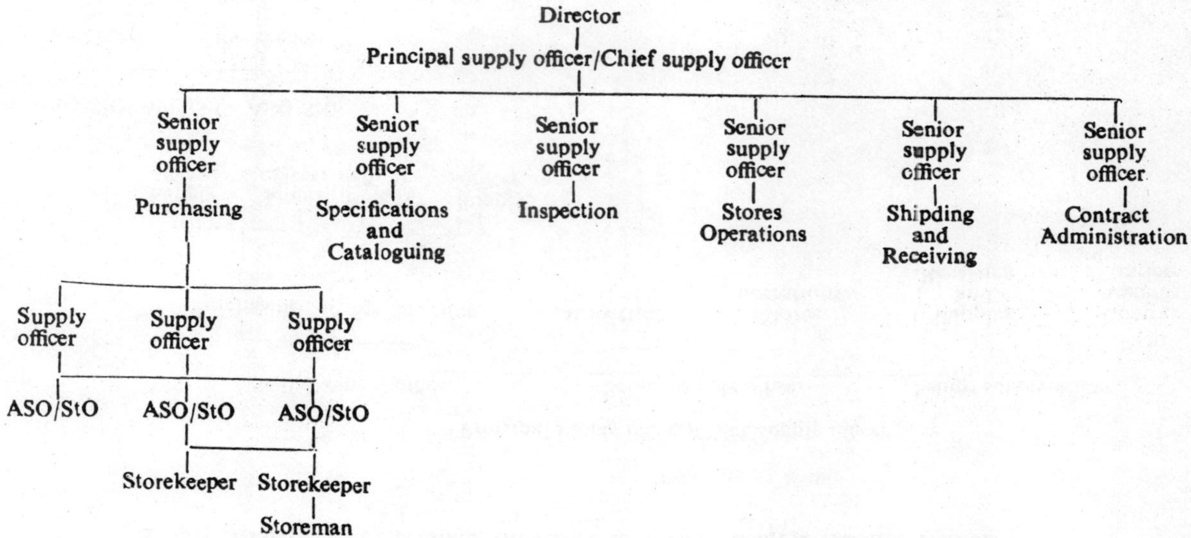

Key: ASO = Asst. stores officer
StO = Stores officer

APPENDIX CHART-9 C

Supply Management Specimen Structure of Posts—Double-function System

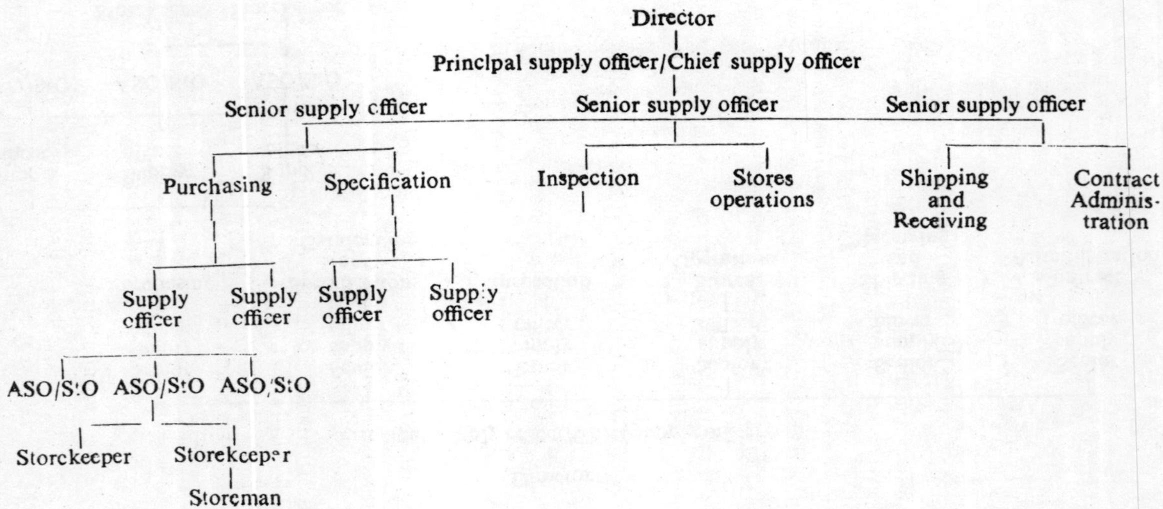

Key: ASO = Assistant Stores Officer

S:O = Store Officer

APPENDIX CHART-9 D

Supply Management Specimen Structure of Posts—Multiple Function System

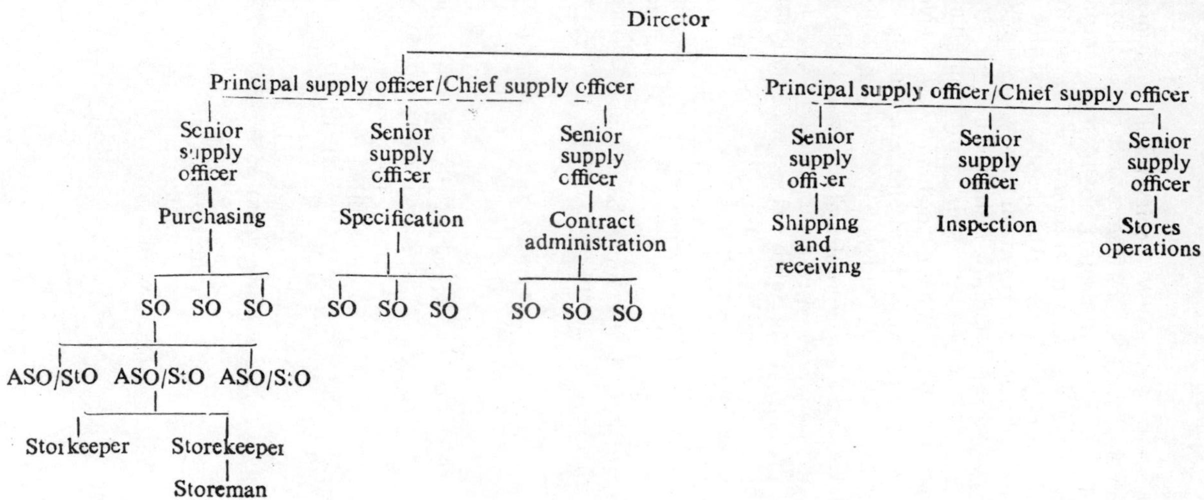

Key: ASO=Asst, stores officer

SO =Supply officer

StO=Stores officer